POVERTY ABOLITIONISTS

POVERTY ABOLITIONISTS

Faith, Activism, and Hope for Difficult Times

DAVID BECKMANN

FOREWORD BY RICK STEVES

BLOOMSBURY ACADEMIC

NEW YORK • LONDON • OXFORD • NEW DELHI • SYDNEY

BLOOMSBURY ACADEMIC
Bloomsbury Publishing Inc, 1359 Broadway, New York, NY 10018, USA
Bloomsbury Publishing Plc, 50 Bedford Square, London, WC1B 3DP, UK
Bloomsbury Publishing Ireland, 29 Earlsfort Terrace, Dublin 2, D02 AY28, Ireland

BLOOMSBURY, BLOOMSBURY ACADEMIC and the Diana logo are
trademarks of Bloomsbury Publishing Plc

First published in the United States of America 2026

Cover design: Diana Nuhn

Library of Congress Cataloging-in-Publication Data Available

ISBN: HB: 979-8-216-27589-3
         ePDF: 979-8-216-27591-6
         eBook: 979-8-216-27590-9

Typeset by Integra Software Services Pvt. Ltd.
Printed and bound in the United States of America

For product safety related questions contact productsafety@bloomsbury.com.

To find out more about our authors and books visit www.bloomsbury.com
and sign up for our newsletters.

CONTENTS

FIGURES

ACKNOWLEDGMENTS

To people in poverty in the United States and many other countries who have been hospitable to me and inspire me.

To the generations of poverty abolitionists who are younger than I am.

To Richard Brown, my editor, and his colleagues at Bloomsbury Publishing, and to Don Pape, my agent.

To Robin Stephenson, who helped me research and write this book. She also developed the graphics.

To Mark Witte, Casey Jones, Richard Nelson, Alice Walker Duff, and Kathryn Brown, who also contributed analysis and research.

To Chang Park, Eleanor Crook, William Moore, Terry Meehan, Carol and Dave Myers, Shep Abell, Maureen O'Leary, and Michael Martin, who have supported my work in recent years.

To Eugene Cho, Eric Mitchell, Heather Taylor, Bob Thompson, Matt Gross, Jamie Thomas, Dave Miner, Sandra Joireman, Kate Pringle, Jeremy Everett, and Lisa Davis, coworkers in Bread for the World and the Alliance to End Hunger.

To Paul Baxley, Galen Carey, Brian Corbin, Amelia Kegan, Chris Kellerman, Walter Kim, Silas Kulkarni, Carlos Malavé, Bridget Moix, Vashti Murphy McKenzie, Jill Rauh, Kerry Robinson, Gabriel Salguero, Julius Trimble, Barbara Williams-Skinner, Adam Taylor, Heather Taylor, Stephen Uram, Jim Wallis, Mary Novack, Ellen Nissenbaum, Heather Valentine, all colleagues in my work with the Circle of Protection.

To Mashal Husain, Max Finberg, Devry Boughner Vorwerk, Anwar Khan, Tom Hart, Maurice Bloem, Susan Marquis, Beth Truesdale, Eric LeCompte, and Sam Daly-Harris, also leaders of the poverty abolition movement.

To Ian Markhan, John Knight, Kyle Lambelet, Ross Kane, Joseph Thompson, Nicky Burridge, Lisa Kimball, and other colleagues at Virginia Theological Seminary.

To Noelle York-Simmons and our friends at Christ Church.

To my wife, Janet, and my sons, Andrew and John.

FOREWORD

by Rick Steves

We need this book now.

David Beckmann was awarded the World Food Prize for his leadership role in the dramatic reduction of hunger and poverty that our country and the world achieved in recent decades. In this book he outlines political and spiritual strategies to get progress against poverty back on track.

As president of Bread for the World, a national advocacy movement on hunger-related issues, David worked to bring Republicans and Democrats together in support of legislation to reduce hunger in this country and around the world. President Trump and his allies in Congress are now eliminating many programs and policies that help families who are struggling with poverty. So David's top priority for us now is to push back, with a focus on people in need.

I'm a traveler and a travel guru. Travel is fun, but it also connects us with people in other countries. It opens our minds to other ways of thinking. European travel that really explores Europe teaches us that government policies can eliminate hunger and provide good health care and schools for everybody—without impinging on anybody's freedom or discouraging entrepreneurship.

Many years ago, a stranger handed me a book titled *Bread for the World*. Ever since reading that book, I've been active in advocacy to reduce hunger and poverty. I've learned that all of us have influence with our members of Congress and that, working together, we can make big changes in policies that are important to people in need.

A few years ago, David helped me make a public television documentary, *Hunger and Hope: Ethiopia and Guatemala*. David and I traveled together through Ethiopia and Guatemala, both very poor countries that have, despite serious problems, managed to make progress against hunger and poverty.

David helped me appreciate the progress they have achieved and learn about ways that the US government has sometimes helped poor people make a better life for themselves and their children.

Together we saw development achievements in Ethiopia and Guatemala that were supported by advocacy campaigns in the United States. For example, we saw how the Ethiopian government had used US food aid to pay farmers to reforest mountains that had been stripped of trees over decades by families searching for firewood. This massive environmental project has increased rainfall in a region that has repeatedly suffered drought and famine. The water table has risen, allowing farmers to irrigate their crops.

US advocates also convinced Congress to expand our government's support for evidence-based child nutrition programs around the world. David and I visited nutrition programs in both Ethiopia and Guatemala. Moms were learning strategies to improve the nutrition of their families, and little children suffering from undernutrition were receiving life-saving nutrition assistance. Despite climate change and increased conflict, child malnutrition has been declining in recent years, partly because of inexpensive, evidence-based programs such as these.

In our own country, national programs like school lunches, WIC, and SNAP have improved child nutrition. US advocates—some of the folks David calls poverty abolitionists—have built and maintained political support for these and other poverty-focused programs over the years.

The Trump administration has slashed US international assistance and pushed for deep cuts in programs that help hungry and poor people in this country. President Trump has also disrupted our economy and threatens our democracy. Continued advocacy with our members of Congress is important. In this book, David Beckmann also outlines other strategies to push back, with a focus on people in need.

After decades of bipartisan work, David now urges us to use our time, money, and influence to elect more Democrats to Congress. He also proposes longer-term strategies to make our politics, our use of the internet, and our nation's religious and spiritual life more generous.

David is a pastor, an economist, and an activist. He brings a lifetime of effective work against poverty to the formidable array of problems that confront our country and the world now.

FIVE INSIGHTS

Insight 1

Poverty Is a Solvable Problem

Our country and the world are facing many problems, but poverty is a fixable problem. I love the chart below (Figure 1) because it clearly shows the dramatic progress of recent decades.

The fraction of the world's population in extreme poverty dropped from about four in ten in 1990 to one in ten in 2024. The fraction of Americans below the US poverty line dropped from three in ten in 1967 to about one in ten in 2024.[1]

Americans are generally skeptical of the government and frustrated by politics. But the US government has played an important role in reducing poverty in both the United States and globally, and active citizens have helped to make it happen. The policies of the second Trump administration are throwing decades of progress into reverse. We need to push back. Action is urgent and will need to be sustained. But we know from experience what works to help individuals and families achieve economic security, and we can get progress against poverty back on track.

Many Americans are discouraged by all the problems our country and the world now face. This book is for people who have a heart for the poor and hope for positive social change. It's for people who haven't focused on changing the politics of poverty before and for experienced leaders and strategists. It will

Figure 1

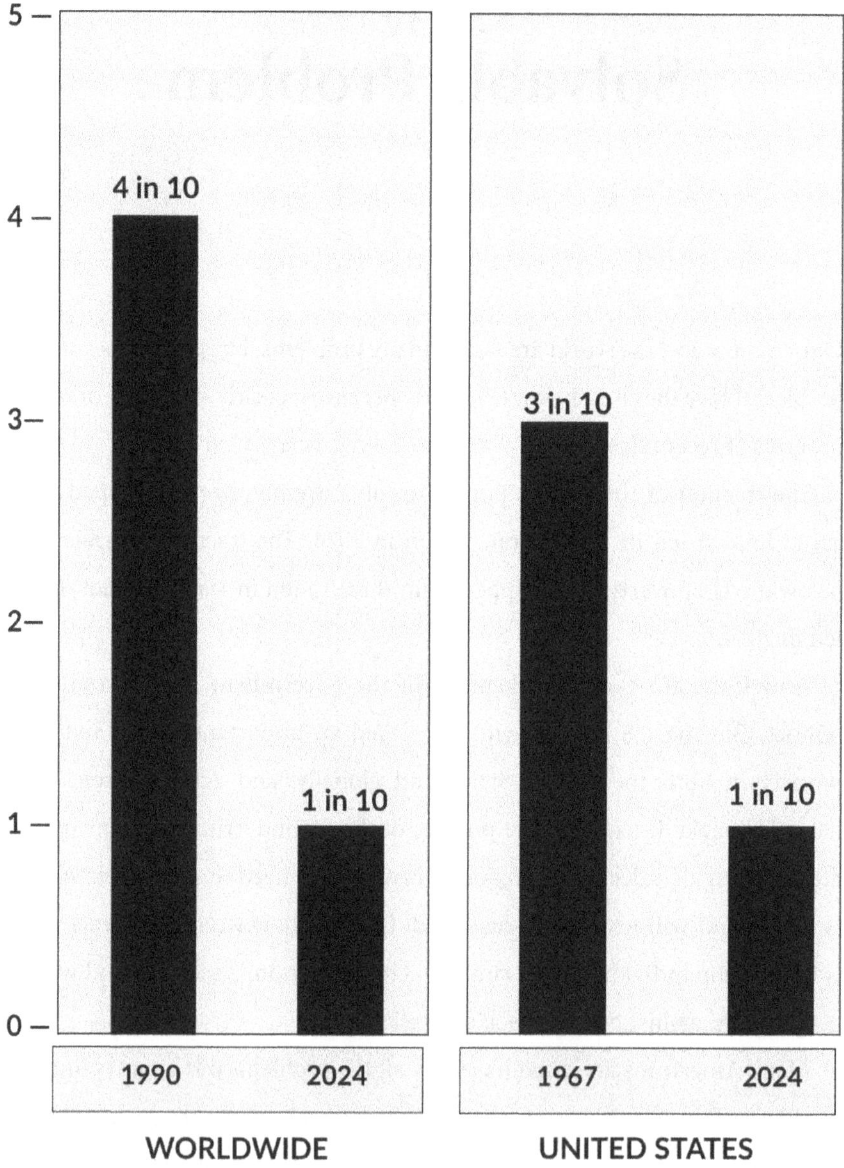

Sources: World Bank, Extreme Poverty; US Census, Supplemental Poverty Measure and, for 1967, estimates from Columbia University.

help you make the most of the time and resources you devote to the cause and may inspire you to do more. In my experience, action to address problems makes us feel better and encourages other people to be hopeful.

Poverty Abolitionists explores political and spiritual strategies that contribute to the political will we need to defend people in need and get progress against poverty going again. Together, efforts along these lines constitute a powerful movement. Our work on poverty issues is, in turn, aligned with the yet broader movement to unravel the knot of problems that our country and the world now face.

No matter what you believe about God or religion, working with others to abolish poverty is clearly sacred work. The historic reduction in poverty pictured in Figure 1 is a great liberation—hundreds of millions of people escaping from material misery. It is like the exodus of the Bible, a contemporary experience of our loving God.

Poverty Abolitionists

Matthew Desmond, author of the *New York Times* bestseller *Poverty, by America,* has called for a stronger poverty abolition movement.[2] This book focuses on various ways to build this movement, drawing inspiration from the movement that led to the end of slavery.

The enslavement of Africans was part of the European colonization of America from its beginning. Laws were developed, starting in Massachusetts and Virginia, to confirm that slaves were property, like cattle. They had no rights and were routinely brutalized. By law, a slave's children and children's children also belonged to the slave owner.

It was difficult for people in slave-holding states to imagine life without slavery—just as it's hard for us to imagine life without poverty in our communities. White people depended on slaves for domestic chores and farm labor. The plantation economies of the southern states were built on slavery. Many preachers found biblical arguments to justify it. Some of the nation's founding fathers had qualms about slavery, but George Washington was the only one who freed his slaves—and they received their freedom only after his death.

A few intellectuals—Benjamin Franklin, for example—were clear that slavery was immoral. Quakers and the early Methodists—both fervent in faith and its implications for social reform—began to organize against slavery.

In 1789, William Wilberforce, a young Methodist member of the British Parliament, launched a long push to pass legislation that would make their slave trade and then slavery itself illegal in the British Empire. A network of activists gradually built up public support through pamphlets and petitions. The movement was ultimately successful, but only after repeated reversals and decades of struggle.

Parliament finally abolished slavery in the British colonies in 1834. The abolition of slavery in the British Empire freed eight hundred thousand people. The United Kingdom was then the most powerful nation on earth and used its influence to urge other nations to help end slavery worldwide.

The US abolitionist movement was led by African American leaders such as Richard Allen, Frederick Douglass, and Harriet Tubman, together with some white Quakers, Methodists, and secular allies. Abolitionists wrote books and tracts, lectured, and organized. Some helped slaves escape to the free states. John Brown led a violent rebellion. Enslaved people themselves developed coping strategies, including churches of their own where they found respite and hope.

The United States was one of the last nations in the world to abolish slavery. When the Constitution was adopted, the Southern states insisted on provisions that made it impossible for the Northern states to end slavery nationwide. As states were added to the Union, the Southern states were able to maintain the balance between states where slavery was practiced and where it was outlawed.

President Abraham Lincoln finally ended US slavery with the Emancipation Proclamation late in the Civil War. He opposed slavery, but his motivation was also partly military. Declaring slaves free further disrupted life in the South, and many of the African American men who escaped to the North joined the Union Army.

During Reconstruction, African Americans experienced rapid advancement in the economy and politics. But within a few years, a new system of repression was established. Jim Crow segregation continued until the Civil Rights Movement of the 1960s. Racist structures continue today, notably laws in some states that discourage African American voting. The proportion of African Americans in poverty is still twice what it is among white people. New forms of human trafficking have emerged. Yet legal, race-based slavery no longer exists anywhere in the world.

The end of slavery made the world a better place. It was an experience of what Jesus called the "kingdom of God" breaking into human history, and abolitionists made it happen. It took the anti-slavery abolition movement almost one hundred years to end slavery in the world.

In our day, it is quite feasible to dramatically reduce—perhaps virtually end—poverty. The economic growth that began in the nineteenth century, combined with social reform, reduced poverty in Europe, North America, Japan, and then throughout the world. Many former colonies became independent nations after the Second World War, and nearly all of them increased efforts to promote prosperity and social development for their people.

In the period between 1990 and now, featured in Figure 1, the world made more progress against poverty than ever before in history. Hundreds of millions of people escaped from poverty. Progress stalled after 2019, and Donald Trump's second term is almost sure to mark the beginning of a period of increasing poverty in the United States and around the world. His administration is attacking immigrants, dismantling protections for disadvantaged groups, and slashing programs for poor people in this country and around the world.

To restore momentum, we need a yet stronger movement of committed people—poverty abolitionists—to push effectively for change in the politics of poverty. People like this can be found in every nation. But we especially need a strong poverty abolition movement in the United States because of its exceptional influence around the world. Matthew Desmond's book called Americans to action, focusing on support for unions, tenant organizations, and other struggles for justice among low-income people. This book discusses a broader array of strategies, beginning with urgently needed change in the federal government. It also discusses needed changes in American religion and spirituality. I'm encouraged by how many people are already pushing to build the political commitment we need to revive progress against poverty and by all the creative ways they are working.

Why Focus on Poverty?

Different people are drawn to different causes, perhaps because of their personal experience with a problem or their sense of what is important. Good causes are usually intertwined rather than competitive, and I encourage you to follow your heart. Most of the strategies this book suggests for changing the politics of poverty are also relevant to related causes.

Yet I want to make a case for focusing on poverty because it isn't the most popular issue right now, even among politically progressive people. As I was seeking a publisher for this book, several editors replied that books about issues, perhaps especially poverty, aren't selling right now. This is partly because many people think that poverty is a hopeless problem. But in fact, we haven't lost the gains against poverty that were achieved in recent decades, and we know from recent experience how to reduce poverty. Poor people themselves also now know a lot about how to overcome poverty, and they are deeply motivated to make life better for themselves and their children.

A second reason to focus on poverty is that reducing poverty can help to unravel the knot of interconnected crises that face our country and the world. Populist politicians mobilize the frustrations of low-income and working-class people to expand their own power. Poor people encroach on rainforests and other vulnerable ecosystems to make a living, and they are usually the hardest hit by changes in climate and extreme weather events. Poverty adds to the sting of racial and gender injustice. It contributes to violence in our country and around the world.

A third reason to focus on poverty is that it is a foundational religious issue. In Jesus's vision of the judgment of nations, he taught that God has a special concern for people who are hungry or thirsty, immigrants, people who can't afford proper clothes, and prisoners (Matthew 25:35–6).[3] The Prophet Muhammad said, "He is not a believer whose stomach is filled while the neighbor to his side goes hungry" (*Sahih al-Bukhari*). One of Gautama Buddha's basic teachings was compassionate action for people in need.

About the Author and This Book

I've had many decades of leadership experience in mobilizing people of faith and conscience to urge our government to help reduce poverty, winning policy changes, and then seeing poverty decline. I served as president of Bread for the World, a grassroots advocacy network of activists and congregations across the country. I was awarded the World Food Prize for our work in support of programs that improved the lives of hundreds of millions of people. I've served as both a pastor and a World Bank economist. I currently lead the Circle of Protection, an advocacy coalition of church bodies and organizations that together have one hundred million members. The Circle of Protection is an important religious voice in defense of the poverty-focused programs of the federal government. I'm also a dean's advisor at Virginia Theological

Seminary, studying and teaching about political and spiritual changes that move us toward the end of poverty.

This book draws on lessons from my own experience to help chart a path for the future. I'm an activist, an economist, and a pastor, so this book is partly an organizing handbook, partly data and analysis, and partly a sermon. Most of this book's readers will be younger than I am, and I look to you to find new ways to tackle today's problems.

Poverty Abolitionists begins with five empowering insights about poverty and how to help overcome it. These are followed by ten effective strategies to build political commitment to end poverty. They include strategies that need urgent attention at this frightening moment in US politics and also strategies that are important for the long-term. Several strategies are ways to reform American religion and spirituality in ways that will make our politics more generous. The final chapter sums up the book, underlining the ethical case for helping to change the politics of poverty and sharing my own faith motivation.

Why a book? Nowadays, we rely heavily on the web to gather and share information. I'm active on YouTube, Facebook, LinkedIn, a blog, and both www.davidbeckmann.org and circleofprotection.org. But a book allows both the author and the reader to think something through in a comprehensive and coherent way. I learned a lot in the process of writing this book, and I pray that you find it helpful.

Insight 2

The Dynamism of People Struggling to Escape Poverty

Most people who are stuck in poverty are fiercely determined to make a better life for themselves and their children. That's one reason why developing countries have, as a group, achieved faster economic growth than industrialized countries. Similarly, disadvantaged people, notably migrants and people of color, have been a source of dynamism in the US economy.

This chapter shares four stories about people climbing out of poverty. I'll start with my own family and then share experiences from very poor communities in different parts of the world. Each of these stories is, in its own way, instructive and inspiring.

Poverty in My Family

Most Americans live comfortably, but a large share of us haven't been able to accumulate enough savings to feel economically secure. Given the uncertainty in our economy and the world, young adults now feel especially insecure. Maybe you or someone dear to you has lived in poverty. Three of my family members have had to deal with poverty.

My mother had to leave home at the age of sixteen. She was part of a Nebraska farm family, and her father was in poor health. They couldn't afford to feed all four of their children, so Mom, the oldest daughter, moved at the age of sixteen to Nebraska's capital city, Lincoln. She helped out in the home of an elderly woman. She managed to save enough money in her first year to give her parents much-needed furniture for their home as a Christmas gift.

Mom never had a chance to go to college. If she had been born a generation later, she could have secured a Pell Grant. Instead, she got married and helped my father move from teaching middle school to administrative positions in small-town school districts, and then to serving as a professor of education at the University of Nebraska. My mother was a talented seamstress, and she eventually led a large program of sewing at Lincoln Technical College. Mom and Dad were able to give their four children a strong start in life, including higher education for all of us.

Both of my sons are adopted. Andrew's birth mother was a graduate student when she got pregnant. She took a break from her studies to have the baby. She didn't have much money and relied on WIC (the Special Supplemental Nutrition Program for Women, Infants, and Children) to provide for her nutritional needs. Andrew is bright and creative, but he might not be as bright if political opponents of low-income programs had succeeded in cutting the WIC program during the Reagan administration.

My son John suffered from severe addiction. He lived in flop houses and dealt with bed bugs. He ended up broke and in trouble with the law. Fortunately, his city has a federally funded drug treatment court that serves as an alternative to prison. They required him to participate in Alcoholics Anonymous and report for drug and alcohol tests. He had to sit in the drug court one day each week for a year, watching as other addicts who had failed to obey the court were sent off to prison.

My wife, Janet, and I gave him some financial support, but not much. We thought that more help from mom and dad would do more harm than good.

Early in his recovery John got part-time work at restaurants. He later sold cell phones in shopping malls. Several of his employers set up complicated systems of paying their workers that allowed the employers to steal wages.

John has now been sober for fifteen years and married for thirteen. He and his wife are deeply committed to their four children. They worked together to make it possible for my daughter-in-law to get a college degree and become a registered nurse. John moved up in business and is now managing a sales staff of eight people.

John knows from experience—and reminds me—that some people end up in poverty because they make irresponsible decisions or just don't work very hard. But he is also an inspiring example of someone who managed to overcome poverty. He got some help from public and private sources, but the success that he and his wife have achieved is mainly due to their own tremendous effort and discipline.

A Friend in Bangladesh

I started my first real job in the northwest corner of Bangladesh in 1974. I worked for the Rangpur Dinajpur Rural Service, funded by the Lutheran World Federation. The organization had started just after the civil war between Pakistan and what became Bangladesh.

Janet and I arrived not long after the end of the war. We lived in Thakurgaon, then a town of about twenty thousand people. I spent several days and nights each week in a tiny market settlement called Gareya. My task was to learn about rural life in Bangladesh and suggest new strategies for our organization. This gave me a life-shaping opportunity to get to know Bangladeshi people, including some very poor people.

When I was in Gareya, I stayed with the local schoolteacher, Mr. Bari, in his thatched house and shared his big wooden bed. In the evenings, two men in the neighborhood would come over, and we spent many hours in conversation about "everything under the sun." But without electricity, we sat in the dark. These friends were patient with my Bengali.

I was able to return to Bangladesh for a couple of weeks in 2011, this time with my son Andrew. We went back to Thakurgaon and Gareya. Bangladesh was still very poor, but much less poor than it was in 1974. The roads were better. The schools were better. There were more fruits and vegetables in the markets, and the children were visibly better nourished.

The women were less confined. Andrew and I met with a self-help group of poor women, and they explained how they worked together to improve their lives. In 1974, women would never have spoken so confidently to a foreign man. Andrew and I went to see the mayor of Thakurgaon, and it turned out that the mayor was a woman! In fact, the prime minister of Bangladesh at the time was a woman!

I got around in 1974 by motorbike, but in 2011 we traveled to Gareya by Land Rover. Gareya had grown into a midsized market settlement, and I had trouble finding Mr. Bari's house. But someone pointed the way, and I spotted him walking by the side of the road. I jumped out of the car, and he walked me back to his house—hand-in-hand, as South Asian men often walk with close friends. His neighbors somehow heard that I was back and arrived about five minutes after we did.

They told me with excitement about improvements in Gareya over the years. The road to Thakurgaon, once a mud road that was impassable during the monsoon season, was now blacktop, and buses ran from Gareya to Thakurgaon and back year-round. The connection to Thakurgaon meant more commerce and better police protection. In 1974, rural households were vulnerable to bandits armed with machetes. Now rural families had some police protection. Mr. Bari had been able to rebuild his house with concrete blocks and connect it to electricity. He eagerly showed me that he had also been able to fill the gully next to the house where mosquitoes used to breed.

I was amazed by all the progress that Bangladesh and my friends had achieved. Toward the end of our reunion, Mr. Bari said, "I thank Allah that our lives have turned out so much better than we expected."

Visit to Mozambique

In 2009, I had the opportunity to visit a very poor area of Mozambique in East Africa. Our first stop was Mtimbe, a settlement of about forty families on the shore of Lake Nyasa—many miles from the nearest road. They had no electricity or running water, and no shops, just mud houses with thatched roofs.

I was traveling with Dave Miner, a grassroots leader from Indianapolis who was serving as board chair of Bread for the World. We flew in a single-engine airplane from the capital of Malawi to a dirt airfield on an island in Lake Nyasa. Waiting for us were Rebecca Vander Meulen, a former Bread for the World policy analyst, and six of her Mozambican colleagues. They were developing what they called "Life Teams" in the Anglican churches of northern Mozambique to help communities cope with AIDS. The Life Teams helped people understand this new plague so they would be less likely to catch it and not blame women for causing it through witchcraft. When medications became available, the Life Teams helped people travel across the lake to see a doctor.

We climbed into a big wooden boat for the trip from the island to Mtimbe. About fifty local people waited for us on shore, singing a praise song, clapping, and moving with the music. The Africans in our boat knew the song and joined in as we neared the shore. Martin, one of Rebecca's colleagues, stood up as we got close. Smiling eagerly, he shouted out the song and pumped his arms to the rhythm. When the boat touched land, he jumped out to hug his Mtimbe friends.

Our hosts pulled our luggage from the boat and led us up toward the settlement, singing and dancing their way up the hill. Mtimbe seldom receives visitors from far away. They carried the luggage on their heads, and Dave and I chuckled to see my big black briefcase, which was usually at home in Washington, D.C., making its way up the path on an African woman's head.

The crowd stopped outside Mtimbe's mud-brick church, and Pedro Kumpila, leader of the local Life Team, formally welcomed us. Rebecca thanked the people for their hospitality and then posed a serious question. She asked the crowd to tell these American visitors how people in Mtimbe had improved their lives in recent years. People paused as they thought about the question.

Someone expressed gratitude for peace. Mtimbe had been repeatedly devastated during Mozambique's sixteen years of civil war. Pedro later told us that he once had to watch soldiers smash a baby in one of the wooden mortars that women use to pound cassava. All of Mtimbe's residents had to flee repeatedly to neighboring countries and live as refugees for years at a time.

The woman carrying my briefcase spoke about Mtimbe's school. They didn't have a school ten years before, but nearly all of Mtimbe's children—even the AIDS orphans—were now learning to read and write.

Pedro noted that AIDS medications had recently become available. Some neighbors who had been at death's door were now able to care for their children, farm, and teach others about AIDS. A few people in Mtimbe even had cell phones that connected to the tower across the lake. Cell phones were a huge advance in a place without roads or motor vehicles.

Mtimbe was still facing big challenges. Each family relied mainly on a little cassava field: if the cassava failed, the family went hungry. Due to turmoil in the global economy, the prices of corn and rice were high, and the government had to cancel plans to bring electricity to the provincial capital.

We met with the entire community as the sun went down. We explained that we were visiting to learn about development in Mtimbe, and the chief and other local leaders introduced themselves. We travelers then retired to

Pedro's mud-brick home for supper, which was chicken and a huge lump of gooey cassava. Later in the evening, I struggled to bathe myself in a thatched bathhouse, fumbling with my flashlight and the bucket of water I'd been given. Pedro and his family stayed elsewhere that night so that Dave and I could sleep up off the ground in their beds.

I climbed into bed and tucked in the mosquito net. As I relaxed and reflected on the past few hours, I was deeply moved by the achievements and hopes of the people of Mtimbe. They are among the poorest people on earth, but they are making strides toward a better life for themselves and their children.

I was also struck by the US government's impact in this remote place. The US Central Intelligence Agency had a hand in Mozambique's civil war. US ethanol subsidies contributed to the high grain prices that people in Mtimbe were facing, and Mozambique's government had to delay investment in the district capital because of the financial crisis that started on Wall Street.

On the other hand, US support for the reduction of Mozambique's debts helped finance schools across the country, including in Mtimbe, and the United States was funding most of the AIDS medications. Bread for the World's members in the United States had helped the people of Mtimbe by urging the US Congress to support debt relief and development assistance for poor countries.

After visiting several other settlements over the next few days, Rebecca and her colleagues took us back across the lake to the island airstrip. Dave, Rebecca, the pilot, and I climbed into another little airplane.

The plane accelerated up the dirt runway, started to fly, but then dropped back to the ground. It veered off the airstrip at sixty miles an hour and bounced violently across a field. The plane stirred up large stones, and one smashed the window near my face. If our plane had stayed on the airstrip for one more second, we would have crashed into a construction site and died instantly.

A couple of weeks later, on a jet headed back toward Washington, D.C., I had time to reflect and pray. The progress that people in Mtimbe had made was a clear example that progress against poverty is possible, and the impact of American government policies in Mtimbe demonstrated the worldwide impact of US politics. The brush with death made me acutely aware that life is short, and I was newly convinced that I should spend the rest of my life working with Americans to get our government to help overcome poverty.

Heartbreak in Ethiopia

This last story is about progress that has been followed by a terrible setback.

A few months before COVID-19 shut the world down, I traveled in Ethiopia with Rick Steves, the travel writer and public-television celebrity. Rick is a dedicated, long-term supporter of Bread for the World, and he was planning a public-television special, *Hunger and Hope: Ethiopia and Guatemala*. He invited me to join him in identifying places where he should return with his film crew.

I have visited Ethiopia five times over the years and was delighted to see again clear evidence that the advocacy of Bread for the World's members for food aid is substantially helping hungry and poor people in Africa.

Rick and I traveled to the Tigray region, which has long suffered repeated famines. In the 1990s, the Ethiopian government began using US food aid to pay farmers to plant trees on the volcanic mountains that had gradually been stripped by families searching for firewood. The farmers also built earthworks to keep rainwater from eroding the mountains. Instead of rushing down the mountains, rainwater now soaks into the ground. The tree cover has also fostered more rain, countering what climate change has done to make drought more frequent and severe in Tigray.

The government also strengthened agricultural research and extension systems with the support of US foreign assistance. Rick and I visited several farm families, including a couple named Abadi and Lela. Because the water table had risen, this couple could now find water under their land for crops and fruit trees. They were able to diversify what they grew on their farm. They set up a waste disposal system that produces methane, so they now have a light bulb hanging from the ceiling of their little house. While they used to sit in the dark at night, they can now see.

In 2022, ethnic conflict—long a problem in Ethiopia—broke into vicious civil war in Tigray and spread to other parts of Ethiopia. The war killed one hundred thousand people in 2022, more than any other war in the world. The war was followed by severe drought.

Renewed violence among ethnic groups has been a terrible setback to Ethiopia's progress. But Ethiopia is still one of the fastest-growing economies in Africa, and poverty continues to decline. Some political leaders, civil-society organizations (including religious bodies), and international actors (notably, the US government during the Biden administration) have worked to reduce violence and address interethnic conflicts.

I was inspired by a group of East African church leaders who came to Washington in 2023 to meet with US government officials and church partners in this country. The delegation included the general secretary of the All Africa Conference of Churches. They explained their ongoing and sometimes successful efforts to train and equip religious leaders as peacemakers at both the national and community levels.

We often find the problems of US politics discouraging. But these East African church leaders are dealing with deeply entrenched problems that are much more severe. Yet they don't give up. They pray, sing, and don't give up. God is inviting us to walk with them.

Insight 3

The Suffering and Harm That Poverty Causes

If you give some thought to how savagely violent poverty is, it may be harder to be satisfied with an individualistic spiritual life.

Poverty in America

Poverty kills people—lots of people. Research from the *Journal of the American Medical Association* shows that sustained poverty is the fourth leading cause of death in the United States. Heart disease, cancer, and smoking are the only risk factors associated with more deaths than poverty. Sustained poverty kills about three hundred thousand people each year. Even short-term poverty significantly raises the risk of a person's death.[1]

Poverty often causes food insecurity and hunger. One in five US families is food insecure—meaning they sometimes have to go without food. Poorer families are often forced to buy inexpensive rather than nutritious food, and mothers often skimp on food for themselves to feed their children. Food insecurity contributes to obesity and crippling diseases such as diabetes and heart disease.

Poor nutrition does irreparable damage to the bodies and brains of little children. If kids don't get to go to preschool, they generally don't do as well in school or in the job market. Schools in low-income neighborhoods rarely give children the kind of education that kids in high-income neighborhoods get. We all suffer when little children aren't able to reach their God-given potential.

The low-income job market is also brutal: temp jobs, gig jobs, part-time jobs, dangerous jobs; low and uncertain wages; wage theft, job loss, and unemployment. The debts of low-income people often compound—late fees, interest charges, and penalties can quickly trap them in a cycle of spiraling debt that is nearly impossible to escape. They are often at risk of eviction or repossession of their car.

People in poverty are often ignored or treated poorly, and they sometimes internalize these assaults on their dignity. They feel like failures. They feel ashamed.

The stress of poverty taxes mental energy and reduces people's problem-solving ability. It leads to anger and sometimes violence—in the home and neighborhood—addiction, and other forms of mental illness. These effects frequently cause trauma in children, further crippling their development.

All of these assaults on health and well-being entail suffering, do great harm, and often lead to early death.

About half of the Americans who are living below the poverty line are white. But African Americans, Native Americans, Latinos, and other people of color are disproportionately afflicted with poverty. They are also much more likely to live in neighborhoods of concentrated poverty—which means concentrated violence, poor public services, and probably no grocery store. While white parents teach their children that police are their friends, African American parents must teach their sons to be afraid and very careful in dealing with police.

Poverty is a threat to most Americans. Many people live in poverty for a while, manage to get ahead a little, and then fall back into poverty. Thirty-seven million Americans (11 percent of the nation's population) were living below the official poverty line ($30,900 for a family of four) in 2023.[2] For an annual report on the well-being of US households, the Federal Reserve asks households whether they have enough cash to cover an unexpected expense of $400. Thirty-seven percent of households say no.[3]

Sixty percent of Americans live in poverty for a year or more and receive public assistance at some point in their lives.[4]

About five million Americans live in *extreme* poverty, comparable to poverty in Asia, Africa, and Latin America. Because of higher prices in the United States compared to lower-income countries, $4 a day in the US is roughly equivalent to the $2 a day definition of extreme poverty that has been used by the United Nations in developing countries. The US official poverty line for an individual in 2023 was $15,000 per year, which is about $40 per day. The five million Americans who live in extreme poverty are subsisting on food stamps and maybe other income worth about one-tenth of that.[5]

Poverty Around the World

The World Bank estimates that 700 million people in the world live in extreme poverty. This estimate is based on periodic household surveys in various countries around the world.[6] Parts of the developing world have recovered from the COVID pandemic and are reducing poverty. But the percentage of people in poverty continues to increase in Sub-Saharan Africa, which now accounts for 70 percent of the global population in extreme poverty.[7]

A growing share (now just over 50 percent) of the people in extreme poverty around the world live in fragile states. These are countries plagued by conflict and instability, such as the Democratic Republic of the Congo (DRC), northeast Nigeria, Sudan, South Sudan, Afghanistan, and Gaza.[8]

We now have multifaceted data on world hunger, which is closely related to extreme poverty:

- 735 million people are "undernourished," which means they are chronically deprived of the calories their bodies need. These people don't have the energy to live fully productive lives.

- 230 million children are malnourished. Thirty-seven million of these children are obese (many in countries where junk food has become widely available), and 190 million are wasted (on the verge of starvation) or stunted (likely to suffer irreparable damage to their bodies and brains).[9]

- 258 million people are suffering from "acute food insecurity" (near starvation), most of them in very poor, violent countries. More than 705,000 people are at the catastrophe level of food insecurity and at risk of starvation—up fourfold between 2016 and 2023. These people are on the edge of famine, with people in Gaza accounting for the largest share.[10]

All the hardships of US poverty—including effects on health and cognitive impairment—are also experienced by people in extreme poverty around the world, but more severely.

The United Nations estimates that fourteen thousand children worldwide still die from preventable, poverty-related causes every day.[11] The number of kids dying from poverty is more than one hundred times the number of people dying from natural disasters—floods, storms, and droughts or heat waves.[12] Yet there's seldom anything in the mainstream news about child mortality around the world, and our response is ho-hum.

Deepa Narayan, a colleague from my World Bank days, led a unique program of listening to people in extreme poverty.[13] Poor people in many countries spoke with teams of local researchers about material deprivation. They also shared experiences of abuse by people in power, the strains that poverty puts on morality, and their hope for their children. Here is a selection of their responses:

First, I would like to have work of any kind.

—An eighteen-year-old man, Isla Trinitaria, Ecuador

Nothing to do during three to four months of rainy/stormy season.

—A group of young women, Ampenan Utara, Indonesia

As if land shortage is not bad enough we live a life of tension worrying about the rain: will it rain or not? There is nothing about which we say, "this is for tomorrow." We live hour to hour.

—A woman, Kajima, Ethiopia

My children are hungry and I tell them the rice is cooking, until they fall asleep from hunger.

—A man, Besda, Egypt

We know that cutting down trees will cause water shortages and that making charcoal can cause forest fires, but we have no choice. Because we lack food, we have to exploit the forest.

—A resident of Ha Tinh, Vietnam

The moneylender and the pawnshop are like husband and wife. One month we borrow from the moneylender and pay the pawnshop. Next month we borrow from the pawnshop and pay the moneylender.

—Participant, discussion group of women, Indonesia

We need boreholes because we rely on unsafe water from streams and unprotected wells. It is a critical problem because most of these streams and wells dry out during the dry season. We have to travel long distances searching for water.

—A participant in a discussion group of poor men and women, Madana village, Malawi

When we fled our homes, we left everything that was of value, all the things that we had worked all our lives to have, to build a home.
—A woman, Bijeljina, Bosnia and Herzegovina

The children keep playing in the sewage.
—A woman, Sacadura Cabral, Brazil

This school was OK, but now it is in shambles, there are no teachers for weeks. It lacks competent principals and teachers. There is no safety and no hygiene.
—Discussion group, Vila Junqueira, Brazil

Because of unemployment, young people drink to excess, commit crime, rape, steal livestock.
—Participant, discussion group of men and women, Ak Kiya village, Kyrgyz Republic

It is because of unemployment and poverty that most men in this community beat their wives. We have no money to look after them.
—A man, Teshie, Ghana

The insufficiency of income is what affects the man-woman relationship. Sometimes she wakes me up in the morning asking for five pounds, and if I don't have it I get depressed and I leave the house. And when I come back, we start to fight.
—A man, Borg Meghezel, Egypt

I worked six years in a company that did not pay me correctly. So I sued them and they threatened to kill me. I had to hide.
—A poor man, Sacadura Cabral, Brazil

The village office turns a deaf ear to our opinions.
—A woman, Harapan Jaya, Indonesia

I do not know who to trust, the police or the criminals. I am afraid that the police might kill my son for something as irrelevant as a snack.

—From a women's group, Sacadura Cabral, Brazil

In the hospitals they don't provide good care to the indigenous people like they ought to; because of their illiteracy they treat them badly.... They give us other medicines that are not for the health problem you have

—Young man, La Calera, Ecuador

If his Bulgarian name is Angel or Ivan or Stoyan or Dragan, he'll get all the application forms and be asked to come in. As soon as he does and they realize he's Gypsy, Roma, he's turned down, they drop their voices and tell him to come some other time.... If you decide to lodge a complaint they tell you, "Who do you think you are, what are you fighting for?" You might be slapped in the face so hard that they'll send you flying through the door.

—Participant, discussion group of Roma men and women, Dimitrovgrad, Bulgaria

We are social outcasts... we are like refuse, like animals. Like a rubbish bin.

—Homeless people in Sofia, Bulgaria

Only God listens to us.

—A participant in a discussion group, Zawyet Sultan, Egypt

The neighborhood association is the only institution that really strives to solve the problems.... It is the only institution that tells us the truth and operates any day, any hour.... The association is close to us, knows the problems.

—Participant, discussion group of men and women, Vila Junqueira, Brazil

Even though life was tough for me, I never gave up hope. I started helping people on their farms in exchange for food. This enabled me to feed my family and even sell some at times. Soon, somebody gave me his cacao farm to look after, and I decided to intercrop the cacao with oil palm trees. This went very well, and when I harvested, I had enough money to start my own farm.

—Neema (age forty-three), Twabidi, Ghana

I live in the hope that things will be better for the children, that they will complete school, learn some trade.

—A poor woman, Sarajevo, Bosnia and Herzegovina

What has most impressed me in my own interactions with people in poverty around the world is their dignity, joy, and persistence. Very poor families generously welcome visitors into their homes and share what food they have. Very poor communities organize festivals with singing and dancing. Very poor people keep striving to improve their situation and, even more intently, to make a better future for their children. In democracies, some poor people actively participate in elections.

Poor people certainly pray, and I'm more sure that God is with them than I am about any other belief about God. Bono, the only rock star I've ever known, said this when he spoke at the National Prayer Breakfast in 2006:[14]

God is in the slums, in the cardboard boxes where the poor play house. God is in the silence of a mother who has infected her child with a virus that will end both their lives. God is in the cries heard under the rubble of war. God is in the debris of wasted opportunity and lives, and God is with us if we are with them.

Insight 4

The US Government and Faith-Based Activists

The future won't be like the past, but we can draw two important lessons from the dramatic progress against poverty of recent decades. First, the US government played an important role in global progress and a crucial role in domestic progress. Many Americans have doubts about the effectiveness of government efforts to reduce poverty, but the record is clear. Second, faith-grounded organizations and advocates helped to get the US government to do what it did. Many people doubt that they can have much impact on national policies, but the record shows that the advocacy of faith-grounded organizations and activists played a key role in the dramatic reduction of poverty between 1990 and 2024.

This chapter explains this history in five sections:

- How the reduction of global poverty in recent decades was achieved and the role of the US government.

- How faith-grounded organizations and activists helped to build US support for global progress against poverty.

- How the US government cut domestic poverty in half during the Lyndon Johnson administration—followed by years of constant attacks and some improvements to the safety net.

- How faith-grounded organizations and activists provided support for LBJ's Great Society and helped to protect and improve safety-net programs in the decades since.

- How the second Trump administration is assaulting poor and vulnerable people, and the need for strong and sustained activism to moderate the damage.

The US Government's Role in Global Progress

The dramatic drop in global poverty between 1990 and 2024 was mainly driven by millions of hard-working families in the developing countries, sometimes supported by the policies of their governments. But several features of the global economy during that period helped to make it possible:

- The global communications revolution made people everywhere aware of what prosperity looks like and the strategies to achieve it—schools, modern medicine, good roads, entrepreneurship, technology, and so on.

- The Cold War ended in 1991 and gave way to a period of relative peace and prosperity.

- Developments in China accounted for a large share of global progress. Universal schooling and health care, followed by increased reliance on free markets and international trade, resulted in spectacular progress against poverty.

US support for progress against poverty around the world also helped make it possible. President John F. Kennedy launched the US foreign aid program in the early 1960s. His inaugural address promised "a systematic attack upon the poverty of the world." The United States encouraged the other industrialized countries to join it in support of international development. But foreign aid was seen as a soft-power weapon in the Cold War against Communism, and US strategic interests often compromised the development effectiveness of aid. Moreover, spending money on foreign aid was not popular with US voters.[1]

A new era in foreign aid began toward the end of the Clinton administration. During the presidencies of Bill Clinton, George W. Bush, and Barack Obama, the United States and its allies in the Group of Seven (G7) took one initiative after another to help overcome hunger, poverty, and disease around the world. Though US foreign aid never rose to much more than 1 percent of the federal budget, the US government's spending on programs of poverty-focused international aid expanded dramatically. It tripled in scale in just the ten years between 2013 and 2023.[2]

The United States also led the nations of the world in the liberalization of international trade. This did harm as well as good, as I'll discuss in the section below about poverty in the United States. But trade liberalization contributed to economic growth in the industrialized countries and opened up new opportunities for people in many developing countries.

Climate change and a growing number of violent conflicts in the world slowed progress against global poverty in the years before COVID. The pandemic shut down the world economy, and global poverty surged. Remarkably, many poor people around the world were able to recover within a few years. The percentage of people in extreme poverty worldwide was about the same in 2024 as it was in 2019. But poverty and hunger continued to increase and become more severe among poor countries afflicted by conflict.

Meanwhile, the United States and other industrialized countries have been increasingly preoccupied with their own problems. The Biden administration seemed less inclined than previous administrations to help resolve conflicts in very poor countries. President Trump virtually ended US international aid during the first month of his second term, and several other industrialized countries cut their aid programs too.

Religious Advocacy Supported
US Leadership for Global Progress

I became president of Bread for the World in 1991. In the 1990s, we were able to win modest increases in funding and pass legislation that focused on improving the quality of international aid. But the Jubilee campaign in 1999 and 2000 was a turning point in political support for poverty-focused international aid.

Several years before, a group of British activists launched an international Jubilee campaign to reduce the debts of low-income countries at the start of the new millennium. The word *jubilee* comes from a passage in the biblical book of Leviticus that calls for all debts to be forgiven every fifty years. In 1999, Bread for the World, a few US church bodies, and Oxfam America developed debt-relief legislation. Christian activists across the country recruited support from their members of Congress.

I love to tell the story about Pat Pelham, a young mother in Birmingham, Alabama.

Pat used her morning walks as a time of prayer, and she felt suddenly called one morning to do something about poverty in Africa. Her Presbyterian pastor noticed that the president of Bread for the World would be speaking at Our Lady of Sorrows Catholic Church, and he suggested that Pat might attend. This led to a "hunger banquet" at Pat's church with their very conservative member of Congress, Spencer Bachus, in attendance.

Later, when Bread for the World was just starting to lobby Congress about debt relief, Rep. Bachus was appointed chair of a key committee. Pat and three friends traveled to Washington to talk with him about debt relief for poor countries. Bachus—a devout Southern Baptist—was moved by what Pat and her friends said about why debt relief for Africa was important to them. Over the next two years, he provided vigorous leadership for debt-relief legislation.

At the White House signing ceremony for international debt relief, I was invited to introduce President Clinton. The president gave Spencer Bachus credit for his leadership, and I used my two minutes to talk about the role that Pat Pelham and other faith-filled activists across the United States had played.

Bono also played a leadership role in securing debt relief for Africa. Although he is Irish, he spent a lot of time in Washington, D.C., because he recognized that an international program of debt relief wouldn't happen without US participation. He generously used his rock-star status to connect with people in high places and to make aid to Africa a popular cause. Bono is a religious poet and a Jesus follower, and his ongoing advocacy is grounded in faith.[3]

The Jubilee campaign started a process that reduced the debt obligations of thirty relatively well-governed poor countries by $78 billion. It cut their annual debt-service payments and increased their annual spending on basic health and education by $3 billion. Debt relief launched a dramatic expansion of school enrollment in Africa, especially among girls.

I don't think all this would have happened if Pat Pelham hadn't been responsive to the call of God during her morning prayers.

Jubilee changed the politics of foreign aid. Bono stayed involved in the United States. He started the ONE Campaign, a secular grassroots advocacy movement for Africa. He convinced Bill Gates to expand what the Gates Foundation had been doing to support Bread for the World and other organizations engaged in education and advocacy on global poverty. The resulting coalition—religious and secular organizations together—built a strong, bipartisan group of members of Congress who kept US support for progress against global poverty expanding year after year, even during the first Trump administration.

I was awarded the World Food Prize in recognition of Bread for the World's role in reducing world hunger during those years.

I also want to flag a more recent advocacy achievement—the spread of research-based child-nutrition programs. Researchers have identified the most effective ways to deal with malnutrition, which kills many children and permanently damages the bodies and brains of a fifth of all the world's children. They have confirmed that focusing on children in the first thousand days of life is most impactful. They learned that nutrition education for parents is an exceptionally cost-effective intervention. RUTF, a high-powered supplemental food, can revive even severely malnourished children.

Bread for the World and partners organization convinced the Obama administration to promote evidence-based nutrition programs for children in the first one thousand days of life (from conception to age two). The United Nations helped to organize nutrition advocates in developing countries. Thanks partly to the proliferation of evidence-based child nutrition programs around the world, the number of stunted children in the world has been declining despite the adverse conditions of recent years. RUTF is saving the lives of millions of starving children.

The US Government's Crucial Role in Domestic Progress

This section is about policy, politics, and their impact on poor people in the United States. It's a story of a strong start, ongoing debate, and some ongoing progress. It doesn't make light reading, but does provide valuable background for poverty abolitionists going forward.

Safety-net programs. Nearly half the decline in US poverty between 1967 and 2024 was achieved by President Lyndon Johnson's Great Society programs. Democrats won the 1964 elections by a landslide and gained big majorities in both houses of Congress. The economy was booming, and Congress further stimulated growth and employment with a tax cut for all income levels.

Under Johnson's leadership, Congress also quickly expanded Medicare, food stamps, and the Job Corps. The Civil Rights Acts of 1964, 1965, and 1968 restricted discrimination and expanded voting rights for African Americans. Congress also set up an array of new anti-poverty programs, notably Medicaid, low-income housing, federal aid to low-income schools, and War on Poverty programs focused on job training and strengthening low-income communities.[4]

A stronger social safety net proved to be an enduring change for the better in our nation. It has been under constant political attack, especially during the Reagan administration and during the first decade of the twenty-first century. But over the years, Congress has maintained and improved safety-net programs, mainly by strengthening their focus on children and incentives to work. The poverty rate has never returned to what it was before the Johnson administration. In fact, debate between the two parties helped to improve the programs—notably, increased focus on children and incentives to work. Mainly because of these reforms, child poverty dropped by 50 percent between 1993 and 2019.[5]

The decline in poverty was slower in the United States than in many other countries, mainly because the growth in US wages has been sluggish since the 1970s, especially for low-income workers. More open trade policies helped raise national income, and we could have used our growing national income for major public investments in the education, health, and welfare of the general population. But we didn't do that. We lowered taxes instead, especially for high-income people. As a result, many working families came to feel that the system is rigged against them.

Policies reduced poverty in the midst of COVID. Twenty-one million Americans lost their jobs when the pandemic began in early 2020.[6] Food banks across the country were overwhelmed. We had every reason to expect a sustained surge in hunger and poverty. But Congress passed a series of massive pandemic relief and recovery bills, mostly on a bipartisan basis. Those bills provided assistance to employers, cash to nearly all families, and targeted aid to vulnerable groups. Poverty dropped in 2020 (the last year of the first Trump administration) and even more in 2021 (the first year of the Biden administration).

President Biden's first major legislation, the American Rescue Plan Act, focused on helping families who were especially hard-hit by the economic effects of the pandemic. It included a major expansion of the Earned Income Tax Credit and Child Tax Credit for low- and middle-income working families. These tax credits supplement workers' earned income, especially for families with children. Thanks mainly to the expansion of the Child Tax Credit among low-income families, child poverty dropped to 5 percent of US children, its lowest level ever![7]

Biden also proposed higher taxes on corporations and on families with incomes above $400,000. This could have avoided an increase in deficit spending, but all the Republicans in Congress joined together to block higher taxes for high-income people.

We decided to let poverty increase again. Tragically, Congress decided at the end of 2021 not to continue pandemic assistance programs for low-income people. Biden and nearly all congressional Democrats pushed hard for an extension of the Child Tax Credit, but it failed by one vote in the Senate in December 2021. Child poverty surged the next month.[8]

Other pandemic assistance programs—expansions of school meals and SNAP food assistance, for example—were also allowed to expire in subsequent months. As these programs ended, communities across the country experienced wave after wave of increased need.

The dip in US poverty in 2021 showed that US government action can reduce poverty. It also showed that we didn't have quite enough political support to reduce poverty permanently. The US poverty rate was allowed to go back up to its 2019 level.

Religious Support for Progress Against Domestic Poverty

Religious organizations and advocates have been stalwarts in support of government efforts to reduce US poverty, mirroring their policy work to reduce poverty worldwide. We need to know the history of these struggles to appreciate the importance of faith-inspired activism now.

LBJ's Great Society program was a response to the civil rights movement, which received important support from churches, mainly African American churches. Most of the Great Society legislation moved through Congress quickly because Democrats controlled both houses of Congress. But Southern Democrats opposed Johnson's civil rights bills, so the religious community focused its advocacy on civil rights.

According to one 1964 report, "The House gallery sometimes seems to overflow with ministers, priests, and rabbis—most of them volunteer watch dogs, who track the votes and other activities of House members."[9] Jim Winkler (former executive secretary of the National Council of Churches) told me that Washington-based advocates would sometimes give church leaders in key districts information about the travel plans of their members of Congress. The local folks would then go to the airport and lobby for civil rights at the arrival gate.

Catholics were a reliable part of the Democratic Party in the late 1960s and early 1970s, and the Social Action Office of the US Conference of Catholic Bishops lobbied for the civil rights bills. The Jewish community also supported the civil rights movement. The groups we now call Evangelical were generally either politically uninvolved or actively opposed to racial integration.

Playing Defense on Domestic Poverty Issues. In the years I was at Bread for the World (1991–2000), the faith community had great success on global poverty issues, but we devoted most of our work on domestic issues to resisting the constant pressure from Republicans to cut poverty-focused programs.

The Circle of Protection (https://circleofprotection.us) came together in 2011, when an expanded Republican majority in the House began pushing for huge cuts in social spending. Every budget passed by either house of Congress between 2011 and 2017 proposed cutting roughly $2 trillion from poverty-focused programs.

The Circle includes Catholics, mainline Protestants, Evangelical Protestants, and African American and Latino churches. We lobby Congress and the president on the big-money bills through which Congress has done most of its business since 2011. Despite repeated government shutdowns and financial brinkmanship, we helped to keep the Republicans from achieving significant cuts to federal anti-poverty programs between 2011 and 2019.

Advocacy by the Circle of Protection, together with other faith-based and secular groups, also played a role in the surprising drop in poverty during the pandemic. In 2020 and 2021, the Circle of Protection supported and helped shape the pandemic response and recovery bills. We energetically supported the American Rescue Plan Act, especially the expansion of the Earned Income Tax Credit and the Child Tax Credit. We spoke up for Biden's proposed increases in taxes for wealthy people on the basis of what the Bible says about wealth and poverty. Finally we also supported the job-creation provisions of the Bipartisan Infrastructure Act, notably the provision of affordable broadband in rural America. When Congress allowed these pandemic provisions to expire, we made sure they knew that poverty was surging because of their failure to act.

Donald Trump's Return to Power

In 2025, Donald Trump became president again. His party controls both houses of Congress, and most of the Supreme Court's justices were appointed by Republican presidents. This time MAGA (the Make America Great Again movement within the Republican Party) was better prepared, so they were able to move forward with radical change quickly. Trump has pushed and sometimes exceeded the limits of what the laws and Constitution allow a president to do. His administration has especially focused on deporting undocumented immigrants, dismantling protections for people of color, and cutting assistance to poor people in the United States and around the world.

Spiritually grounded people are called—by God and by our consciences—to push back against MAGA policies and defend people in need. Extra effort is urgently needed. The Republican Party is likely to pursue the policy directions of Trump's first year back in office through the end of his term and well beyond.

Insight 5

A Huge Setback and Hope for the Future

We've traced the history of how US government policies aided or slowed progress against poverty in past decades. This chapter focuses on the MAGA policies of the second Trump administration and on policies that could lead back toward the end of poverty in a more favorable political situation. It includes a section on data we can use to track results. Finally, it closes with a discussion of how our efforts to reduce poverty are interconnected with the threats to democracy, climate change, and the other menacing problems that our country and the world now confront.

MAGA Policies

I'm writing this book near the end of the first year of President Donald Trump's second term. The policy directions below are likely to continue through the end of this administration and perhaps beyond. They will increase poverty in the United States and internationally.

Domestic assistance program cuts. Trump has unilaterally stopped or curtailed scores of poverty-related programs. Republican majorities in both houses of Congress passed his "big, beautiful bill." It made massive and permanent cuts to Medicaid, SNAP, and other social programs. It also included big tax cuts—mostly for high-income people—and massive deficit spending.

Deportation and discrimination. An often brutal program of mass deportation is imposing huge costs on many struggling families who have risked everything and worked hard to reach a decent standard of living. The administration has also reversed systems that protected civil rights and curtailed discrimination against African Americans and other disadvantaged groups. It has eliminated programs that promoted diversity, equity, and inclusion.

Economic mismanagement. Increased deficit spending will weaken confidence in the US dollar and US bonds. Trade wars and tariffs are likely to slow economic growth for years to come.

International assistance cuts. US international aid amounted to about 1 percent of the federal budget, yet it kept tens of millions of people alive, helped to reduce poverty, and enabled many to build lives with dignity. This administration has slashed international aid and destroyed USAID. These actions have crippled health and development efforts around the world and contributed to deadly hunger in some countries.[1] On a visit to South Africa in 2025, I learned that eight thousand skilled health workers were laid off when the United States stopped supporting HIV-AIDS care—and that US tariffs were expected to eliminate a hundred thousand jobs.

Destructive US leadership in the world. President Trump has undercut international alliances that the United States has led since the end of the Second World War. His bullying style of international diplomacy has yet to bear much fruit. His administration has also abandoned international efforts to curtail climate change. All of this has dramatically and perhaps permanently weakened the United States' capacity for positive influence on other governments.

Right-wing authoritarian government. This administration, supported by our conservative Supreme Court, argues that the US Constitution authorizes yet more power for the US president. This ideological framework has allowed President Trump to unilaterally end many government policies and programs. He has also been able to use the power of government to attack his personal and political enemies. The threat that MAGA poses to democracy is a threat to all Americans, and right-wing authoritarian governments tend to be especially bad news for minorities and low-income people.

Policy Directions That Would Restore Progress Against Poverty

If elections result in different leadership, we could move in new directions, which include policies that provide help and opportunity to poor and vulnerable people. Figures 2 and 3 outline policy directions that would, in my view, foster progress against poverty in our country and around the world.

This policy wish list is ambitious but not radical. Nor is it expensive compared to other things that our government does—big tax cuts for wealthy people, for example. Assistance policies are obviously important for progress against poverty, but social, economic, and diplomatic policies matter as well. Many of the policy directions I'm suggesting would help working-class and middle-income people as well as people in poverty. Our government's policies should foster opportunity for all Americans.

In 2015, the nations of the world all committed to end poverty by 2030. If we can mobilize the political commitment needed to pursue a policy agenda along the lines of Figures 2 and 3, we could still get to the end of poverty in our country and around the world by 2040.

Figure 2

POLICIES THAT COULD VIRTUALLY END POVERTY

In the United States

1. Create jobs that pay.

The best way to end poverty is to make it possible for people to secure good, family-sustaining jobs.

- Manage the economy to promote growth and employment. Reduce deficit spending and restrictions on trade. Raise revenue by reversing tax cuts on corporations and high-income people.

- Expand work supports, including child care and paid leave.

- Raise the minimum wage and increase the Child Tax Credit, especially for families in poverty.

2. Strengthen the safety net and invest in people.

- Ensure that everyone has access to health care, nutrition, education, and housing.

- Make voting easy for everyone, including people of color and low-income people.

3. Remove obstacles to earning a decent living.

- Reform the immigration system to control the border, facilitate legal immigration, and allow undocumented people a path to citizenship.

- Enforce laws against discrimination in the job market.

- Eliminate racial discrimination in the legal justice system.

Figure 3

POLICIES THAT COULD VIRTUALLY END POVERTY

Around the World

1. Provide U.S. leadership for international systems that reduce poverty.

- Practice democracy (a free society, the rule of law, and voting rights) and promote it worldwide.

- Promote peace and security—including peace processes in fragile states—addressing the root causes of forced migration.

- Do our part to slow climate change and help low-income countries cope with it.

- Encourage international trade, with protections for vulnerable people.

2. Provide finance for international development.

- Rebuild organizational capacity and restore funding for health, development, and humanitarian assistance—with a focus on countries suffering from conflict and/or famine.

- Establish international bankruptcy procedures to provide debt relief to countries that are struggling with impossible debt (an idea that Pope Francis promoted).

Tracking Results

The first page of this book draws hope from data on poverty trends over many years. Data helps us moderate our optimistic or pessimistic moods. It also allows us to hold ourselves and governments accountable for results. Governments have a responsibility to maintain good data on poverty, and poverty abolitionists need to have some knowledge of key sources of data on poverty.

The best US poverty data comes from the Census Bureau. The original US poverty line, developed in the 1960s, was based on a minimal food budget with an allowance for other basic needs. The Census Bureau continues to gather data on poverty as it was originally defined, but since 2009 it has also published a supplemental measure that is more accurate in several ways. Notably, it counts government assistance as income. This book cites poverty data according to the Census Bureau's improved measure.[2]

The incomes of low-income Americans are often unstable, with many people living above the poverty line for a while and then dropping below it again. The group just above the poverty line is sometimes called "working class," and that's the terminology I use.

The most reliable data on global poverty comes from the World Bank. The Bank's definition of extreme poverty was originally based on what it would cost a family to afford enough of a basic staple (such as rice) to provide the calories their bodies need. This is a much more severe standard than the US poverty line.

The United Nations also maintains data on hunger, which is closely related to poverty. The US government maintained data on hunger in America until the Trump administration decided to stop.[3]

In 2015, the nations of the world jointly committed to the Sustainable Development Goals to end poverty and improve environmental protection. They also set specific targets for sub-goals—improving educational results, for example—and agreed on quantitative indicators to track progress. This led to the development of a much more comprehensive system of data on human welfare around the world, including the status of women in different countries.

The Trump administration has weakened data collection and analysis on social and environmental issues in various ways. Doing our best to keep track of what's happening among poor people is now more important than ever.

One final thought about data. In religious and ethical traditions "poor" clearly has a more general meaning than any of the technical measures social scientists have developed. The God of the Bible is especially concerned about people in need generally.

Reducing Poverty and the World We Want

The world is now faced with interlocking crises: stalled progress against poverty, economic uncertainty, runaway climate change, an increase in violent conflict, a surge in authoritarianism, and widespread spiritual malaise.

Dysfunction in one area contributes to dysfunction in others. For example, the world's failure to slow climate change has led us into an era of more destruction from heat waves, floods, fires, hurricanes, and tornadoes. That's been bad for the economy and disastrous for many families—especially low-income families. Violent conflicts are contributing to severe hunger in a number of countries. They have also disrupted the global economy and fueled the worldwide trend toward authoritarian government.

Figure 4 pictures the good we seek in response to each of these interrelated crises: peace, democracy, prosperity, declining poverty, environmental sustainability, and shalom (spiritual peace).

Poverty is a problem on which progress is clearly possible, and (as mentioned in the first chapter, Insight 1) it would contribute to progress on the other big problems we face. Some specific examples:

Figure 4

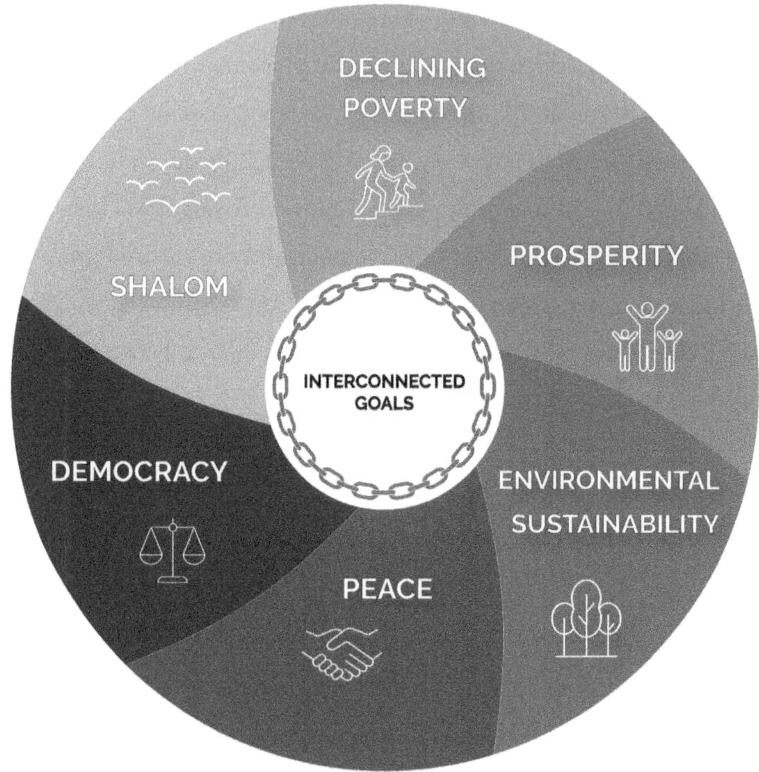

- Higher incomes for people in poverty would contribute to prosperity for everybody.

- Progress against poverty would also reduce the harm from weather events since families in poverty often live in vulnerable but affordable locations.

- Progress against poverty would certainly reduce violent conflict.

- It should also strengthen democracy. Higher incomes lead to better-educated citizens. Also, conservatives and liberals are sometimes drawn to work together on poverty-related issues—hunger among children, for example.

- Finally, progress against poverty would be good for our souls.

The US government and United Nations don't gather data on shalom—a Hebrew word for wholeness, completeness, and peace with God—but it's an important aspect of what makes the world good.

The brokenness of our country and world has led many people to turn inward—toward fear, anger, or indifference. But shalom invites us to turn outward and upward, opening ourselves to God, to one another, and to a larger vision of the good. Hope and love are deep in the human psyche and may power the effort we need to move toward the world we want. In the New Testament, hope and love are seen as gifts of the Spirit of God.

One way to embrace shalom is by engaging in efforts to regain progress on poverty. Working for justice can be a spiritual practice.

TEN STRATEGIES

Strategy 1
Legislative Advocacy Works

In the first five chapters of this book, I've discussed five foundational insights for activism to revive progress against poverty:

- Poverty is a solvable problem, and many people are working to overcome it.

- The determination of people struggling to escape poverty is especially impressive.

- Poverty causes tremendous suffering and harm.

- The US government and faith-grounded activists played important roles in the reduction of poverty over recent decades.

- Current US policies will increase poverty, but an alternative set of policies could get us back on track toward ending poverty.

This is the first of ten chapters that focus on effective strategies for poverty abolitionists. These strategies are opportunities to engage in the cause. You might be drawn to two or three serious commitments and also weave a few less time-consuming changes into your life. You may also be inspired by the many ways individuals and organizations are contributing to the movement to overcome poverty. If you believe in God, you may recognize all these efforts together as God moving among us toward the end of poverty in the United States and worldwide.

I know from experience that legislative advocacy works. In the chapter on the US government and people of faith (Insight 4), I offered examples of successful advocacy in which I was personally involved. Over the years, I have repeatedly witnessed teachers, pastors, retirees, students, parents, religiously motivated people, and people with lived experience of poverty speak out and move lawmakers to action. Even in today's very difficult political landscape, all kinds of people—not only policy experts or political insiders—are pushing to shape the laws, policies, and priorities of our society.

Advocacy Works Even Now: A $500 Million Surprise

Advocating for the interests of people in poverty is more difficult now than ever before in the thirty-five years I've been active in legislative advocacy. As discussed in the chapter on policies (Insight 5), President Trump and his supporters are doing tremendous harm to people in need in the United States and around the world.

But surprisingly, legislative advocacy was able to achieve two significant wins during Trump's rapid-fire attack during his first months back in the White House—a $500 million increase for WIC (nutrition assistance for infants, small children, and their mothers) and the restoration of $400 million for PEPFAR (HIV/AIDS assistance in Africa).

$500 million for WIC. In March 2025, the new Republican-dominated Congress passed an appropriations bill for the final six months of the 2025 fiscal year. It cut assistance programs by $13 billion and, worse, expanded the president's authority to shift money from one purpose to another—in effect, authorizing the administration's Elon Musk-style attacks on government departments. Still, this bad bill, developed and passed by Republicans only, also included an extra half-billion dollars for WIC.

How did that happen? The process was a bit complicated, but worth studying step-by-step. There are two storylines that come together with the passage of this bill.

The main plotline begins with the fact that WIC is an exceptionally effective program. To qualify for WIC, women must have evidence of need and a medical prescription. WIC pays only for foods that are nutritionally important for young children and lactating women. The moms receive nutrition education as well as groceries. WIC has demonstrably reduced premature births in the United States. It saves tax dollars, because groceries are a lot less expensive than it costs Medicaid to cover hospital care for premature babies.

The proven success of the program has fueled decades of effective advocacy on the part of Bread for the World, RESULTS, the Food Research & Action Center, the National WIC Association, and the agriculture and grocery interests that benefit from the food purchases that WIC finances. Bread for the World and RESULTS have repeatedly mobilized grassroots campaigns for WIC, and all the groups in the WIC advocacy coalition have consistently worked on both sides of the aisle in Congress.

In late 2023, a group of Right to Life organizations started lobbying for WIC. Right to Life organizations have traditionally focused entirely on making abortion illegal, but some of them are now also advocating for programs that keep babies alive and healthy after they are born. These groups are trusted among Republicans, and they helped solidify Republican support. Pro-WIC Republicans include Vice President J. D. Vance, Senate Majority Leader John Thune, Speaker of the House Mike Johnson, and Representative Tom Cole (chair of the House Appropriations Committee).

Over the years, Republicans and Democrats have come to agree that they will approve the funding needed to provide WIC to all the eligible women and children who apply. But only about half of the families eligible for WIC do apply, so the Department of Agriculture made a major effort during Biden's administration to make WIC more attractive to eligible families. Notably, they made it possible for families to connect with WIC remotely rather than having to visit a WIC office in person. Participation increased. At the same time, food prices rose. Because of these changes, the Department of Agriculture informed the White House that WIC would need an additional $500 million in fiscal year 2025 to provide help to all the eligible families likely to apply.

As Congress developed the six-month appropriations bill, the White House sent them a list of needed changes from the previous appropriations bill. Amazingly, the Trump White House put the extra $500 million for WIC at the top of their list. I'm not sure who was responsible, but it probably didn't hurt that Vice President Vance is supportive of WIC.

The other plot line starts early in 2024, when Bread for the World (now led by my successor, Eugene Cho) decided to include WIC as a focus of its 2025 advocacy agenda. That mobilized more advocacy support for WIC from Bread for the World's big grassroots network.

Bread targeted some members of Congress who would be influential in the appropriations process. One of their targets was Representative Robert Aderholt, a senior member of the House Appropriations Committee. He would certainly be consulted as decisions were made about funding for WIC. His district in Alabama has a higher percentage of Republicans than any other district in the country.

In early 2024, Bread for the World organizer Florence French traveled to Jasper, a town in Aderholt's district. She met with staff of the Jasper Area Family Services Center. Florence invited them to send a few people to Bread for the World's advocacy summit. At this Washington gathering, these people had their first experience as public policy advocates.

When they returned to Jasper, one of them, Makenzie Brown, met with Aderholt's local constituency service representative. At Makenzie's invitation, that staffer visited the Family Services Center.

"We talked with her about what we're seeing every day," Makenzie later told me, "and pitched the improvements Bread for the World was seeking in WIC and the Child Tax Credit."

Makenzie herself has experienced poverty. Her mother wasn't able to take care of a child, so her grandparents adopted her. They struggled economically, and the family qualified for free school lunches. She has now finished college and, at the age of 27, has become an effective anti-poverty abolitionist.

In late 2024, Makenzie called her contact in Aderholt's office and invited the congressman to speak at the public launch of Bread for the World's 2025 campaign. She explained that he would be expected to make a specific commitment to at least one of the programs Bread hoped to improve. The event took place at the US Capitol in January 2025. Makenzie flew back to Washington for it, and she introduced Aderholt. Two other Republicans were also among the legislators who made commitments that evening.

Aderholt had voted in 2023 to freeze WIC funding rather than adjusting it to meet expected needs. But perhaps in part because he was hearing from constituents in Jasper, he did not object to the big increase of 2025. Makenzie checked with her contact in his local office and sent me a text, "Great news! He did vote yes for the WIC increase!"

She is now engaging other people in advocacy—five women who are using WIC, the staff of her agency, and the director of adult education at the local community college. She also participates digitally in Hunger Free Alabama, which focuses on hunger issues in the state legislature.

$400 million for PEPFAR. One of the first things President Trump did in his second term was an executive order that paused all the United States' international assistance, and USAID was the first target of Elon Musk's DOGE (the so-called Department of Government Efficiency). DOGE staff walked into USAID, managed to take control, and quickly dismissed almost all USAID staff.

A strong coalition has long been active in support of international assistance—US Global Leadership Coalition, Global Health Council, Bread for the World, the ONE Campaign, InterAction, and many other groups. They worked together to protest the destruction of US international assistance. The Global Health Council sued to reverse the abrupt dismissal of USAID staff, won in the lower courts, but lost at the Supreme Court. The press reported the story, focusing on deadly impacts in many developing countries. One study estimated that the cessation of US health assistance would lead to fourteen million deaths in five years.

The coalition intensified advocacy with Congress in July, when the Trump administration formally requested a rescission of $9.4 billion in previously appropriated funds. Almost all of the $9.4 billion was international aid. Some faith groups in the Circle of Protection who don't usually focus on international aid also spoke out and activated their networks.

Senator Susan Collins, chair of the Appropriations Committee, convened a hearing, and seven Republican committee members expressed support for aid programs that the administration had cut. Collins and a few other senators developed an amendment to the rescissions bill, the White House agreed to it, and the amended bill passed both houses of Congress. It restored $400 million to PEPFAR and instructed the administration to continue five other aid programs that had been discontinued.

Features of Effective Advocacy

Advocacy helped win an extra $500 million for at-risk children and $400 million to help HIV/AIDS patients in Africa in the midst of an administration and Congress otherwise intent on slashing anti-poverty programs. This is evidence that advocacy sometimes works even in the most difficult environments. Below are lessons for effective legislative advocacy, drawn in part from these narratives.

Contacting your members of Congress makes a difference. Emails and letters to your representative and senators make a difference. The Congressional Management Foundation advises congressional offices on management issues and has, in the past, surveyed members of Congress and their senior staff about communication from constituents. One survey revealed that it typically takes fewer than fifty personalized emails on an issue to spark action from the congressional office.[1] In another survey, more than 90 percent of staffers said that personal communication from constituents (in-person visits, letters, or personalized emails) has a lot of influence on the members of Congress they serve. I've seen it myself many times: when folks back home weigh in, members of Congress pay attention.[2] Big campaign contributors have undue influence, and the two political parties put pressure on their members to follow the party line. But people back home who contact their member of Congress get heard, because members need their votes to stay in office.

I recommend Sam Daley-Harris's book, *Reclaiming Democracy: Every Citizen's Guide to Transformational Advocacy*, for training in effective advocacy. It teaches advocates to be ambitious about what they can achieve. It also teaches practical skills, such as how to develop an elevator pitch of no more than two hundred words that powerfully communicates an advocacy message.[3]

It helps to be part of an advocacy organization. You are likely to have more impact if your advocacy is part of an organized effort. The advance planning that Bread for the World staff did for their 2025 campaign set up an exceptionally impactful advocacy opportunity for Makenzie Brown.

Bread for the World includes more than three hundred thousand people, including at least one active leader and one active church in every congressional district. So Makenzie knows that her ongoing advocacy in Jasper is in partnership with what thousands of like-minded activists are doing in all parts of the United States. Florence French and other Bread organizers support these advocates. Other Bread staff complement what grassroots volunteers can do. For example, the government relations staff is in routine contact with coalition partners and congressional staff.

Bread for the World is as strong as it is partly because it enjoys support from thousands of donors, including some who make very large gifts. Their generosity supports staff salaries and the other costs of effective advocacy.

Relationships. The most effective advocates develop relationships with their elected representatives. Makenzie has developed a personal relationship with a staff member in the office of her member of Congress.

I've built a relationship with my congressional representative, Don Beyer. He has come to my church a couple of times over the last year, and I grabbed the chance both times to ask about the issues I'm working on. He helped me get a meeting for the Circle of Protection with Hakeem Jeffries, the Minority Leader of the House of Representatives.

I respond to Beyer's fundraising appeals from time to time. If he is making a speech at a fundraising event and sees me in the room, he's almost sure to mention hunger and poverty. He cares about hunger and poverty, but when he sees me, he's reminded that he also has constituents who care.

Bipartisanship. US voters are almost evenly divided between the two parties, so compromise and collaboration between them are usually needed to pass legislation, and certainly needed to make changes durable. Advocacy with members of Congress on both sides of the aisle makes sense, and congressional offices pay attention to all constituent communication.

For more than a decade, almost all congressional Republicans have voted repeatedly for deep cuts to poverty-focused programs, and President Trump's leadership has made them more extreme. So I'm now doing everything I can to elect Democrats to Congress. But I continue to be in conversation with Republicans and am heartened that all-Republican decision-making processes supported an expansion of WIC and the protection of PEPFAR.

Coalitions. Strong coalitions supported the 2025 increases in WIC and PEPFAR. The diverse church bodies and ministries in the Circle of Protection work together because it makes them more impactful than they would be otherwise.

Sustained effort. Policy change doesn't usually come quickly. Members of Congress are knowledgeable people and have well-developed views on many issues. It often takes a year or two—sometimes much longer—for a bill to work its way through Congress. Implementation of big decisions also takes time. A major, durable change in the world may require a series of legislative successes over a period of years. This doesn't happen without persistent advocacy by people and organizations committed to getting it done.

Advocacy also takes a certain amount of faith. The wins may seem small—a committee vote that blocks a harmful provision in a big bill, or an amendment that makes a modest improvement to an anti-poverty program. Sometimes you are just planting seeds and trusting that someone else will see them bloom.

Churches and charities. Churches are powerful, mainly because they are full of voters. Churches are an important part of the Bread for the World network. Their members write thousands of letters to Congress each year. I love it when church ushers bring baskets of letters to Congress up to the altar along with financial gifts from the congregation.

Charities are widely respected and understand community needs. That's why Aderholt's staffer asked to visit the Jasper Area Family Services Center.

Churches and charities are an important part of the constituency for government action to reduce poverty and on some other issues. One snag is a common misunderstanding of Internal Revenue Service regulations on churches and charities. Nearly all nonprofits and houses of worship register with the IRS as 501(c)(3) organizations. This confirms the tax-deductibility of contributions. IRS rules include no restrictions on what churches and charities say on social and policy issues. Churches and charities can also lobby elected officials on specific legislation, as long as lobbying isn't a substantial share of their total activity. Very, very few houses of worship or charities come anywhere near devoting a substantial share of their budget to lobbying.

The IRS rules are explained in IRS Publication 1828, *Tax Guide for Churches & Religious Organizations.*[4] The Alliance for Justice offers a short fact sheet titled *Lobbying Rules for Houses of Worship.*[5]

The power of faith and morality. When people urge their members of Congress to support effective anti-poverty programs, they speak with moral and sometimes religious authority. In my experience, most members of Congress are decent people, and the doors of power sometimes open unexpectedly.

Advocacy at the State and Local Levels

Federal decisions often have big, long-lasting effects, and my experience has been mostly at the national level. But advocacy at the state and local levels is also important.

Republicans are currently more dominant in state legislatures than in Congress. The number of governors from each party is about the same. In all but twelve states, the governor works with a legislature in which their party has the majority.[6]

The Constitution leaves it to state governments to establish voting procedures for both state and federal elections, and voting rights have been a matter of debate in state legislatures in recent years. Blue-state legislatures have been making it easier for people to vote. Red-state legislatures have been making it harder, often targeting African Americans and other vulnerable categories of voters. In 2025 President Trump convinced the Texas state legislature to redraw the lines of congressional districts to favor the Republican Party. This started a gerrymandering competition between Republican- and Democratic-majority legislatures. If your state legislature is considering a change in legislation related to voting, it could be a high-impact opportunity for advocacy.

City councils play an outsized role in making affordable housing and public transit available.[7] City councils and school boards set policies for public schools (teacher salaries, for example). Local decisions such as these often have direct impacts on families struggling with poverty.

A variety of advocacy organizations work in state capitals: church groups, multi-issue groups, groups focused on voting rights, child-focused groups, racial justice groups, and environmental groups. At the local level, community organizations, local institutions, neighborhood associations, and individuals all weigh in on policies.

Advocacy by People Who Have Lived It

People struggling with poverty are usually preoccupied with their own problems. Someone trying to figure out how to put food on the table for their kids just doesn't have time to help fend off threats in Congress to future funding for WIC—let alone think about possibilities to improve child nutrition around the world. Thus, it's important for other people to learn about and speak up on these issues.

But when people with lived experience of poverty have opportunities to engage in legislative advocacy, they bring firsthand knowledge and urgent passion to the work. They are an inspiration to all of us. I'd like to tell you about two friends who have translated their past experiences of poverty into powerful advocacy and successful careers.

Dawn Pierce. Dawn first attended Bread for the World's annual gathering in 2013. She is a resident of Boise, Idaho, and I had the privilege of joining her meeting with Republican Senator Mike Crapo, the senior senator from Idaho. I was impressed that she was given a meeting with the senator himself rather than with one of his staff. The population of Idaho is relatively small, and relatively few constituents come to meet with their members of Congress in Washington, D.C.

That year, SNAP (the Supplemental Nutrition Assistance Program) was in Republican crosshairs, with the goal of cutting benefits for millions of people and removing the program from the Farm Bill. Senator Crapo was calling for deep cuts and damaging structural changes to SNAP.

Dawn told Senator Crapo about her own experience with SNAP. Dawn was a nurse, but she lost her job during the Great Recession. While she looked for new employment, she needed SNAP to feed herself and her teenage son. At the same time, she was managing type 2 diabetes—made more difficult on a SNAP diet. The health and financial strain was difficult enough, but the shame she felt was overwhelming. She never thought she would need help to take care of her family. She described sitting in her car crying before she could bring herself to ask for help.

"I was pretending not to be scared in our meeting with the senator," Dawn later told me. "But then I noticed that he had tears in his eyes."

When the final bill—without cuts to SNAP—came to a vote in early 2014, he voted the way Dawn had wanted.

This was Dawn's first experience as an advocate. But she continued to advocate with Bread for the World and, over time, with other anti-hunger organizations too. "I've grown so much from what I've learned through advocacy," Dawn told me in a recent conversation.

She has come to know many of Idaho's elected officials at the federal, state, and local levels. She sees Senator Crapo two or three times a year. When they saw each other at a recent event, she introduced herself. "Oh, I know you," he replied. "You're the hunger and food lady."

Two years ago, Dawn was hired by Hunger Free America. She now serves as their national director of organizing and community empowerment. She is also board chair of the Idaho Hunger Relief Task Force. Dawn has made a run for the Idaho state legislature and plans to run again.

Barbie Izquierdo. I first learned about Barbie from a documentary film about hunger in America called *A Place at the Table*.[8] Back then, she was a struggling single mother. But she was determined to make a better life for herself and her children. She has written down the story of her life.[9] She reports candidly about growing up amid poverty and violence, and about the years when she and her two little children often had to go without food.

Barbie connected with community organizations and was able to find work. She counseled other women, learned to speak up for herself, and was asked to speak at public events. After the release of *A Place at the Table*, she was invited to travel to events where the film was shown. From Barbie's memoir:

> When opportunities came to speak on panels, join community discussions, or contribute to research, my first instinct was to doubt myself. Who was I to be in these spaces? But I learned to silence that doubt with one word: Yes.
>
> And every time I said yes, doors opened.... I went from being a mother struggling in silence to a leader shaping conversations around hunger and poverty.

Barbie has testified before Congress. She helped to organize a White House Conference on Hunger, Nutrition and Health, and she is currently director of neighbor community engagement for Feeding America, the nationwide network of food banks. She is an advocate on policies and also works with organizations to help them understand the importance of listening to the people they are trying to help.

Strategy 2
Elections Shape the Future

Elections are important. They shape the future, and our two main parties envision very different futures for our country and the world. Democrats and Republicans are almost evenly balanced, and almost every national election shifts the balance of power.

Legislative advocacy cannot, by itself, fend off funding cuts and policies that increase poverty. We need to strengthen the voice of the opposition party. Independents and Republicans might consider voting for Democrats at this juncture.

Elections are especially important now, because our country's democracy is at risk (as discussed in the next chapter). The best way to protect democracy is for voters to weigh in. Since President Trump and Republican legislatures are changing election rules in their favor, we may not have another opportunity to change directions for the foreseeable future.

Securing a Democratic majority in one or both houses of Congress in 2026 would, to some extent, constrain President Trump. For the sake of vulnerable people, it is essential that we elect a president and Congress in 2028 who will move us toward a more hopeful future.

If the Democrats win big in the next two or three elections, we're likely to see reforms in the Republican Party. Many working-class voters are now Republican. Some Republican leaders are already urging the party to align their policies more closely with the interests of working-class people by reducing their taxes and protecting health care. I dream of the day when the parties are debating how to expand opportunity for low-income and working-class people.

Attitudes Toward Electoral Politics

Nowadays, political passions run deep. Many people are outspoken on issues—especially on social media. Most people strongly identify with one side or the other. Different parts of the country are liberal or conservative, and some people decide where they want to live partly on the basis of whether they will be surrounded by other people who have political attitudes similar to theirs. Many of us have little contact with people on the other side of the political divide. The clothes we wear, the foods we prefer, and the cars we drive vary according to whether we lean liberal or conservative. Fifty-five percent of churchgoers say that their political views match those of most of the people in their church.[1]

Yet relatively few people are seriously engaged in elections. Only about two-thirds of eligible voters turned out in each of the last three presidential elections.[2]

Only 2 percent of US adults give more than $200 to candidates, parties, or PACs during a two-year election cycle.[3] Based on the Cooperative Election Study, only 28 percent made any financial contribution to a candidate in 2020, and that dropped to 20 percent in 2024.[4] These numbers are shockingly low, and it is striking that the share of adults contributing to candidates dropped in 2024—which turned out to be what may be the most consequential election in many years.

Other types of involvement in elections are also low, and were lower in 2024 than in 2020. Only 4 percent of US adults worked for a candidate in 2024, 5 percent in 2020. Fifteen percent put up a political sign in 2024, 19 percent in

2020. Indicators of political participation more generally—contacting a public official or attending a political meeting—are also low, and they were lower in 2024 than 2020.[5]

Why Aren't More People Actively Engaged in Elections?

A Pew Research Center survey in 2024 found that more than eight in ten Americans believe that elected officials don't care what people like them think. That's true for Americans of all sorts: men and women; white, African American, and Latino; all ages; all levels of education; Republicans and Democrats; and people whose engagement in politics is high or low. Most Americans think that lobbyists, special interests, and wealthy donors have too much influence. Sixty-three percent of Americans feel that elected officials run for office to make money; 15 percent feel that elected officials get into politics to serve the public.[6]

I've worked with many elected leaders, and most of them—even those with whom I disagree—are conscientious people and dedicated public servants. But I agree that money has way too much influence in politics.

This has always been a problem. Mark Hanna, President William McKinley's 1896 campaign manager, famously said, "There are two things that are important in politics. The first is money—and I can't remember what the second one is."[7]

But this problem has become much worse. Since the 1970s, lobbyists have raised money from special interests in exchange for favors, skirting rules that prohibit this.[8] In 2010, the Supreme Court's *Citizens United* ruling opened the floodgates to unlimited funding from wealthy people and corporations. There are limits on a donor's contributions to parties and candidates, but wealthy individuals and corporations are now able to give as much as they want to

PACs or so-called "outside organizations" that work alongside campaigns. Some of these organizations are not required to report their sources of funds, allowing big donors to contribute "dark money."[9]

The 2024 federal elections—presidential and congressional races together—cost $15.9 billion, up from $8.5 billion in 2016 (mainly because so much is now at stake). A few donors made huge contributions—notably, the $277 million that Elon Musk gave to Donald Trump.

We need campaign finance reform. But Republicans have managed to block reform in both Congress and the Federal Election Commission since 2010. Congressional Democrats tried to pass election reform legislation in 2022. It included campaign finance reform provisions, such as tighter restrictions on PACs and quicker decisions from the Federal Election Commission on violations of election rules. But this bill failed to pass the Senate by two votes, with all Senate Republicans voting against it.[10]

Giving Money

There are various ways we can influence elections, but I want to start with giving money. Why? Because I think that increasing financial support for candidates who are aligned with our values is one of the most urgent and important things we can do to push back against MAGA and revive progress against poverty.

To reduce the dominance of super-wealthy donors, more Americans need to give money to candidates, with higher-income people contributing in proportion to their means. If more Democrats are elected, they will restrain Trump and perhaps reverse some of the harm he has done to poor and vulnerable people. If more Democrats are elected, we will also have a better chance of getting campaign finance reform.

The percentage of US adults contributing to politics is low, but has increased over the last fifteen years.[11] This is a trend we need to accelerate, especially for candidates who will help end poverty. We also need more people who give a significant share of their income to political candidates.

You can contribute to candidates you would like to have represent you at the local, state, or national level. They need money to get elected, and your donations will also help you build relationships with them—like I have done with my member of Congress.

You can also contribute to your favored candidates in competitive elections across the country. Or you can give to a party committee, such as the Democratic National Committee, the Democratic Senatorial Campaign Committee, or the Democratic Congressional Campaign Committee. These party committees direct funds they receive to the activities and races where they will have maximum impact.

You might also consider supporting an organization that is focused on an election-related purpose other than the victory of one candidate or another:

- Quite a few organizations focus on getting more people out to vote. These include the Poor People's Campaign and Rock the Vote. The Brennan Center and the ACLU work to expand voting rights. Others work to protect at-risk voters from violence and intimidation at the polls—Faiths United to Protect Democracy, for example.

- Some organizations use elections as an advocacy opportunity. Bread for the World has urged candidates from both parties to make commitments on hunger-related issues. The Circle of Protection coalition managed to get almost every candidate for president between 2012 and 2020 to make a short video on what they would do to provide help and opportunity to hungry and poor people. Ominously, we couldn't get either Trump or Biden to make videos about poverty in 2023 or 2024. The Circle isn't set up to receive tax-deductible contributions, but you can follow its work at circleofprotection.us.

- Finally, an organization called American Progress is pushing for a constitutional amendment that would overrule the Supreme Court's decision on *Citizens United.* This is a long shot: Congress would need to approve a constitutional amendment, and thirty-six states would have to ratify it. But American Progress and its supporters have already convinced twenty-six legislatures to urge Congress to pass the draft constitutional amendment that American Progress is proposing.

Other Ways to Be Effective in Elections

The candidate who raises more money than their rival usually wins. One study found that this held true in eight out of ten Senate races and nine out of ten House races.[12] But money isn't enough. Notably, Biden and Harris together raised twice as much money as Trump in the 2024 presidential race. Nevertheless, Trump won the election. Clearly, factors other than money are influential, and there are other ways to help win elections.

Voting. It all comes down to voting. It's important to vote and to encourage friends, family, neighbors, and associates to vote.

Primary elections let every voter help choose their party's general-election candidate. But it doesn't make sense to stay home from the polls if we're not enthusiastic about either of the candidates on a general-election ballot. Staying home has the same result as voting for the candidate you oppose.

I'm excited that a growing segment of the electorate is Gen Z and Millennial voters. James Sergio Crocker, a seventeen-year-old activist, points out that Gen Z voters are progressive, almost half of them are people of color, and their voter turnout rate is high.[13]

Influence people in your network. Most people's thinking is shaped mainly by other people in their network—family, friends, neighbors, colleagues, groups to which they belong, and people with whom they are connected on social media. Advertisers have learned that the best way to sell something is to get people talking about it within their networks.

Talking about political issues with family and friends helps us clarify our own thinking and that of those close to us. But we need to be careful not to waste time and energy doomscrolling and lamenting the state of our nation's politics.

You might make a plan to influence how people in your network will vote in the next election. Focus on four or five people you hope to influence.

A yard sign or a campaign button or shirt advertises your views and can also spark conversations with neighbors or people you encounter as you go about your day.

Volunteer for a campaign or your party's local headquarters. Campaigns need people to go door-to-door, preferably talking with their own neighbors. They ask volunteers to make calls, send postcards, and staff tables at the farmers' markets. It's fun, necessary, and builds the volunteer's knowledge, commitment, and relationships.

Go to a rally. Rallies deepen commitment and enthusiasm.

Pray. I pray for my community, our nation, and the world, especially for people in need. I pray by name for people in public office and those seeking public office. I pray for people in my network whom I'd like to vote differently in the next election. Prayer changes things. Most obviously, it humbles us and aligns our lives with the Lord's Prayer: "Let your kingdom come, let your will be done on earth as in heaven."

Reinhold Niebuhr's "Serenity Prayer" is another prayer for our time: "God grant me the courage to change the things I can, the serenity to accept the things I cannot change, and the wisdom to know the difference."

The vocation of churches. Pastors and churches should prayerfully consider a more active role in the coming elections.

What's most widely known about churches and elections is that IRS regulations prohibit 501(c)(3) organizations, including nearly all churches, from endorsing parties or candidates. But IRS regulations explicitly allow churches and charities to provide nonpartisan voter education (candidate forums, for example, or discussions on ethical and religious values that underlie the current political debate). Churches clearly can participate in voter registration or get-out-the-vote drives and encourage their members to play an active role in elections. On this as well as on questions about lobbying, see the IRS Publication 1828, *Tax Guide for Churches & Religious Organizations*.[14]

The current Trump administration's IRS has indicated that they don't think the rule against endorsing candidates applies to churches—that pastors speaking to their congregations are like a family discussion. But most churches will probably continue to avoid endorsing candidates or parties, because the rule is still on the books. Also, churches need to be careful about partisan passion dividing their community or crowding out religious teaching.

Yet churches, synagogues, and mosques should be doing more than they have done to discuss the moral and religious issues in politics. They can and should:

> preach and teach about the values and beliefs at stake in the nation's political debate;

> encourage people to be active—and generous—in shaping elections, stressing that contributions to candidates are an aspect of good stewardship;

> participate in efforts to encourage and protect voting, especially among people of color and low-income people; and

> organize opportunities for people to discuss election issues in a civil way.

Relatively few religious communities are as effective as they could be in influencing the outcome of elections. Moses, Samuel, the prophets, and Jesus all addressed political leaders and spoke about political issues. I pray that religious leaders will speak out—loud and clear—at this critical time in our nation's life.

Strategy 3
Defending Democracy

The second Trump administration has raised alarms about preserving the rule of law, the freedoms Americans enjoy, and democracy. Our country has moved toward what might become a right-wing authoritarian system of governance—expanding executive power, weakening oversight, and silencing dissent.

Presidents have overstepped constitutional authority before. Richard Nixon, for example, abused federal power—including withholding funds appropriated by Congress—and ultimately had to resign. During the First World War, Woodrow Wilson used the Espionage Act to censor media and jail political opponents. Andrew Jackson defied the Supreme Court to force the removal of Native American communities from their homelands. Yet in all these cases, despite serious overreach, our institutions—flawed as they are—held, and the constitutional balance of power was eventually restored.

This administration's abuses have been more expansive. To a great degree, President Trump has ruled the country by decree. Federal law enforcement and justice agencies have been stacked with loyalists and weaponized against perceived enemies. This administration has attacked universities and law firms, picking them off one by one, leading others to "pre-obey"—to conform to the administration's policies to avoid becoming targets. Loyalty has been rewarded with access, favors, or pardons, and Trump has used his position to enrich himself.

Everyone living in the United States is protected by the Bill of Rights, which guarantees core civil liberties such as freedom of speech and due process. Yet this administration has repeatedly—and at times brutally—disregarded the rights of immigrants, including those lawfully present in the country. Undermining due process threatens the freedoms of all of us and opens the door to broader abuses, including censorship. More generally, our government has switched from defending the civil rights of historically disadvantaged people to defending white people from discrimination.

Voting, the cornerstone of a democratic government, is also under attack. Trump has issued an executive order to reshape election rules in ways that benefit his own party. Since the Constitution doesn't give the president authority over election rules, Trump's allies in Congress have developed legislation that mimics his executive order. He has urged Republican-majority state legislatures to redraw congressional districts to partisan advantage, and some legislatures will make it harder for people to vote in future elections.

The threat to democracy is much bigger than one man. Very few elected Republicans have spoken out against these abuses. The Republican majority in Congress has unanimously approved nearly everything the president has requested. Federal courts have ruled that many of the executive orders were illegal, but the Supreme Court has generally sided with the president. Across the country, millions of people have repeatedly voted for Donald Trump and other MAGA Republicans. No matter the outcome of the next few elections, the anti-democratic tendencies that are now so immediately threatening will continue to be a powerful force in our society.

The Founding Fathers looked to the American people to protect democracy. This chapter explores what that defense looks like: lessons from history and other nations, the importance of maintaining the integrity and independence of US institutions, and practical steps that people of faith and conscience can take. In our time, defending democracy is an essential aspect of the push to renew progress against poverty.

Understanding Authoritarianism

Over the past decade, authoritarianism has surged globally, and the United States is not immune to this trend.[1] Nicolás Maduro in Venezuela and Recep Tayyip Erdoğan in Turkey are entrenched strongmen who have dismantled democratic checks and silenced dissent. But increasingly, it's not just dictators who pose a threat to democracy. Viktor Orbán in Hungary and Javier Milei in Argentina are recent examples of freely elected leaders who leveraged democratic weaknesses, often under the pretext of a national emergency, to erode the very institutions and norms that enabled their rise to power.

Orbán, a right-wing nationalist, was elected prime minister of Hungary in 2010 and remains popular with the voters who brought him to power. His party won a slim majority of the popular vote, but Hungary's election rules gave his party more than two-thirds of the seats in Parliament—enough to amend Hungary's constitution. That expanded authority gave Orbán the power to undermine democracy, weaken judicial independence, and curtail press freedom.

Elon Musk wasn't the first to wield a chainsaw onstage as political theater—Javier Milei of Argentina did it during his campaign. Once in office, he followed through, slashing welfare programs, firing tens of thousands of public employees, and cutting aid to soup kitchens. Within a year of his inauguration, poverty in Argentina surged to more than 50 percent of the population.

For background on the progression and perils of authoritarianism, I recommend a Rick Steves documentary. In *The Story of Fascism in Europe*, Rick explores how people's dissatisfaction with dysfunctional governments and runaway inflation led to the rise of autocrats like Hitler, Mussolini, and Franco in the aftermath of the First World War.[2] All three of these "strongmen" rose to power by promising to restore national pride and greatness, using people's frustration and fear as a pathway to power. Like many modern dictators, Hitler came to power through elections and subsequent legal manipulations.

Protect Democracy, a nonprofit dedicated to defeating authoritarian threats, developed this list of seven tactics that have been repeatedly used by autocrats and would-be autocrats. They named it "the authoritarian playbook"[3]:

- Politicizing independent institutions

- Spreading disinformation

- Aggrandizing executive power

- Quashing criticism or dissent

- Scapegoating vulnerable communities

- Corrupting elections

- Stoking violence

The movement that President Trump now leads has employed all of these authoritarian tactics, including attempts to corrupt elections and stoke political violence. When Trump falsely claimed he had won the 2020 election and encouraged a mob of his followers to storm the US Capitol, he crossed a line no American president had before.

Reinforcing Pillars of Support

The Constitution divides government power among three branches and between the federal and state levels, providing a system of checks and balances against the abuse of power. The move toward authoritarianism requires support from these other institutions of government.

Autocrats also need the cooperation of civil society: faith communities, businesses, professional associations, and universities. Maria Stephan of the Horizon Project argues that power flows upward through such institutions. She calls them "pillars of support."[4] It's powerful when they push back, especially if they rally together to defend an institution that a would-be autocrat has attacked.

Poland offers a hopeful example of the successful defense of democracy.[5] In 2015, Poland began sliding toward right-wing authoritarianism. After a few years, the government attempted to purge the independent judiciary. A broad-based pro-democracy movement emerged in response. They mounted a nonpartisan civic effort to educate the public and restore democratic norms and values. Members of the judiciary went directly to the people, using plain language to explain what was happening and how it would affect their rights, freedoms, and daily lives. Civil society organizations launched their own public education efforts. These actions invoked widely shared values and included citizens who had once supported the party in power. They helped shift public opinion and shaped the next election, restoring democratic governance.

One of the core insights of Stephan's work is that you can't defend democracy unless you include those who supported its erosion in the first place.[6] The same lesson applies in the United States. Many of the people who voted for Donald Trump didn't do so out of a love for authoritarianism—they did so because they believed the system was broken and wanted change. The vast majority of his supporters believed he would fix Washington and improve an economy that had left them behind.[7] Trump's narrative made them feel seen and heard.

Pushback against the harsh features of Trump's presidency began early: Bishop Mariann Budde used her sermon during the Inaugural Prayer Service at the National Cathedral to ask Trump for mercy, humility, and a commitment to justice. Pope Francis denounced inhumane deportation tactics, calling the mistreatment of vulnerable communities a moral failure. Federal workers who lost their jobs without due process shared their stories on social media—stories that were amplified by ordinary citizens, journalists, and advocacy groups. Senator Cory Booker spoke on the Senate floor for twenty-five hours about the harm being done to the most vulnerable under the Trump agenda, reaching a national audience through this spectacle of sustained moral witness.

Individual actions like these matter. But perhaps even more powerful is collective action that shows broad, unified resistance across divides. Already in 2025, millions of people took to the streets in a series of mostly nationwide, mostly nonviolent protests.

To further resist the rise of authoritarianism and strengthen the pillars of democracy, ordinary citizens can take concrete actions: we can urge our members of Congress, especially Republicans, to exercise their independence and resist President Trump's relentless push for power. We can give financial support to organizations—such as the ACLU—that urge the judicial system to restrain Trump's overreach and defend the Constitution. And we can urge state and local governments to refuse to comply with some of Trump's diktats.

Effective Responses to Defend Democracy

Democracy is strongest when people show up together. The Civil Rights Movement was the greatest pro-democracy movement in the history of the United States, and it relied on collective action: teach-ins, boycotts, nonviolent protest, and strategic use of media. It exposed the injustice of segregation and Black disenfranchisement, reframing these issues as fundamental violations of democratic rights. Churches and faith communities served as organizing hubs and moral anchors, helping to galvanize a movement rooted in justice and dignity. This movement shifted the national conscience and forced the United States to reckon with the gap between its ideals and its reality. These tactics can be employed again.

Nonviolent movements are more inclusive and more effective than violent resistance. Much of what follows draws on the work of organizations like the Horizons Project and Protect Democracy, which serve as hubs for antiauthoritarian research, resources, and organizing. These are some of the most effective tactics being used today to defend democracy:

Religious resistance. Check out Jim Wallis at the Georgetown Center on Faith and Justice, Adam Taylor at Sojourners, and/or Dr. Barbara Williams-

Skinner at The Skinner Institute. They are all leaders of Christian resistance to the threats of Christian nationalism and the rise of right-wing authoritarianism. Together, they are organizing a series of actions that respond to current events and protest the harm that Trump and his allies are doing to poor people, Black people, and immigrants.

Civic education. Teach-ins, community forums, and storytelling campaigns help people understand what's happening and how authoritarian policies affect their lives. Clear, relatable language is key to changing hearts and minds. Democracy Circles—a guide for small groups—offers advice and materials to help synagogues, churches, and other groups engage people in thinking about the current challenge to democracy and then take action together.[8]

Direct action. Peaceful protests, marches, sit-ins, prayer vigils, and occupations draw public attention, expose injustice, and force confrontation with systems of power. Groups like Hands Off and Indivisible have been instrumental in organizing protests against budget cuts that impact low-income and middle-class communities. Sojourners and Bread for the World have led prayer vigils in support of poverty-focused programs.

Noncooperation. Refusing to comply with unjust demands—through strikes, boycotts, and student walkouts—can extract too great a cost for perpetrators to continue. Labor unions are powerful civic forces against authoritarian systems. Universities can use their endowments to maintain programs despite cuts in federal funding. Boycotts can pressure business leaders to speak up. Pastor Jamal Bryant launched a boycott of Target to oppose its rollback of initiatives to promote diversity, equity, and inclusion.[9]

Creative resistance. Art, music, and satire can challenge propaganda, inspire solidarity, and make movements more accessible and engaging. Humor is also an important tool. Making a joke in the face of authoritarianism takes courage—and inspires courage.[10]

Digital organizing. Social media, messaging apps, and livestreams allow for rapid mobilization, storytelling, and coordination—especially when traditional media or institutions fail to speak out. If you subscribe to media outlets that are holding authoritarian leaders accountable—such as the *New York Times* or *The Atlantic*—you can share articles to spread trusted information.

Legal action. Legal challenges and watchdog efforts can delay or block authoritarian power grabs and document abuses that erode legitimacy. These lawsuits often rely on individuals willing to speak up, even at personal cost. When nonprofit organizations sue the government for abusive action, we can support them financially. It's expensive to go to court.

Authoritarian systems rely on fear to keep people silent. Threats of violence, job loss, or public shaming are being used to discourage dissent. But silence gives those in power permission to continue. That's why it is critical that good people—especially those in trusted institutions—speak up against threats to democracy.

Now and in the years ahead, some people will need to suffer loss, perhaps prison, to protect democracy. But courage is contagious. When one person takes a stand, others are more likely to follow.

Mr. Rogers once said, in times of trouble, look for the helpers. They may be in your local church or among the organizations listed in this book—groups that can help you take part in the kind of collective action that defends democracy. Or maybe you'll be the one to start something new. What matters—for progress against poverty and our collective future—is that we act when faced with authoritarian threats, before it's too late.

Strategy 4
Struggles for Justice

This chapter is about organizations that focus both on the needs of marginalized groups and on organizing people in those groups to speak for themselves. It's not easy for someone who is struggling to pay the bills to find time and energy to push for social change. But many low-income people do just that, and the organizations in which they play leadership roles are important to the politics of poverty.

Racial-Ethnic Organizations

African Americans, Latinos, and Native Americans are all disproportionately affected by poverty. Systemic injustice has led to a poverty rate among African Americans today that is twice that of their white counterparts. Yet Black communities have built an array of strong institutions to address community needs and defend their interests.

These include national civil rights organizations like the NAACP and the National Urban League. The NAACP (National Association for the Advancement of Colored People) has defended the interests of African Americans since 1909. It pushes on issues of economic development—housing and broadband access are high on their priority list—and voting rights. The Urban League has a similar agenda but devotes more effort to business development and training in the communities it serves.

African American churches are also important in the fight for Black justice. Black Christianity has served as a center for social change and a driving force in the struggle against injustice. In many underserved communities, the church is a source of help to the most vulnerable and an ally to secular social justice organizations. It is also a hub for community organizing.

Black Lives Matter is a movement that has changed American culture. Three young Black women—Alicia Garza, Patrisse Cullors, and Opal Tometi—launched it in 2013. When George Zimmerman was acquitted in the shooting death of African American teen Trayvon Martin, their hashtag, #BlackLivesMatter, went viral on social media. A year later, another Black man, Mike Brown, was killed by police in Ferguson, Missouri. Activists from eighteen cities organized Black Lives Matter chapters in their home communities. In response to a need, the Black Lives Matter Global Network was launched to empower millions of Black voices all across the country.[1]

Black Lives Matter contributed to a broader racial reckoning. It included widespread awareness of the brutal and long-term consequences of slavery and Jim Crow; prompted decisions across the country to take down monuments to Confederate leaders; and spurred controversial efforts to reduce racial discrimination in policing and the justice system. It was in this context that many corporations, nonprofits, and the federal government launched diversity, equity, and inclusion (DEI) programs.

For the Hispanic community, UnidosUS supports civil rights and advocates with a network of more than three hundred community-based groups across the country. Through voter registration efforts, public education, and policy campaigns, it helps raise the voice of Latinos as a voting bloc that deserves attention. Latinos make up a large share of the labor force but earn a significantly smaller share of the nation's income. UnidosUS has been a strong advocate on Capitol Hill against cuts to SNAP and other safety-net programs that would hit Latino families especially hard.

Traditionally, most Latinos have voted for Democrats, but 46 percent of Latino voters cast their ballot for Trump in the 2024 elections. Since most

Latinos are either Catholic or Evangelical, opposition to abortion runs high among them. After that, economic issues, including health care and safety-net issues, are high priorities. Many Latinos who voted for Trump thought he would give them a stronger economy, and some supported his promise to end the influx of undocumented immigrants. This political complexity highlights the importance of Latino-led organizations like UnidosUS.

Latinos are a substantial and growing share of the Catholic community, and the US Conference of Catholic Bishops is a strong voice on immigration issues. The National Latino Evangelical Coalition (NALEC), which includes more than three thousand Hispanic evangelical congregations, speaks out on poverty, immigration, and family issues from a faith-based perspective.

Native communities have also often been sidelined in policy discussions, even though they have suffered centuries of unjust federal policies. Many Indigenous people live on tribal lands with limited access to resources, jobs, and health care, leading to the highest poverty rates in the United States. Their strongest representatives are the tribal governments. Native communities also organize through local and national groups such as the Native American Rights Fund. The Native Organizers Alliance blends traditional values with a community organizing approach.

The second Trump administration has been chaotic for Indian Country. Funding cuts have been announced, then rescinded, then partially implemented anyway.[2] Notably, the administration moved to defund tribal colleges and other educational programs for Native people. The Native American Rights Fund filed a lawsuit on behalf of three tribal nations and Native students, arguing that the cuts to tribal colleges violate treaty obligations and federal law.[3]

Faith-Based Community Organizing

Community organizations take many forms—from professional organizations that represent community interests, to coalitions that bring together diverse stakeholders, to community organizing groups that train and bring marginalized communities together to advocate for policies that are important to them. Most community organizing is focused geographically, but some of it is focused on groups with shared interests—tenants, for example. The model I know best is faith-based organizing, focused on organizing marginalized people with support from religious organizations.

For more than fifty years, the US Conference of Catholic Bishops and some mainline Protestant church bodies have invested in a nationwide network of faith-based community organizing. It began with Saul Alinsky, an organizer on the South Side of Chicago in the 1960s. The Industrial Areas Foundation (IAF), founded by Saul Alinsky, uses a method of organizing that builds durable political power and influence through churches, schools, and other neighborhood groups. Their approach emphasizes relationships among people with shared goals—face-to-face conversations, leadership training, and then collective action to win concrete improvements in people's lives.

With strong support from church bodies and increased support from foundations, IAF and Faith in Action—the two most prominent faith-based organizing networks—have helped launch organizations in about two hundred communities across the United States. Together, these local groups include around 4,500 member institutions, the majority of which are religious congregations—mainly Catholic, mainline Protestant, and African American churches. These networks have developed a strong, tested approach to organizing and helped many low-income people grow as leaders and advocates.[4]

They have also won many policy victories at the local and state levels. IAF reports, for example, that its affiliates in Texas, Arizona, and Louisiana have won public funding for labor intermediary organizations that provide long-term training and help connect job-seekers with employers. These intermediaries have helped sixteen thousand people move from poverty-level jobs to living-wage careers.

East Brooklyn Congregations, an IAF affiliate, pioneered a strategy that has replaced hundreds of acres of blighted, abandoned housing with large-scale developments of new, high-quality, affordable housing for low- and moderate-income residents of those communities. Since 1983, about seven thousand homes have been constructed in New York, in Baltimore, and Washington, D.C.—transforming some of the nation's most blighted urban communities.[5]

Faith in Action focuses especially on issues of importance to people of color—police reform, for example, and it is helping undocumented immigrants deal with mass deportation. One of its affiliates, Faith in New Jersey, helped win passage of state legislation that allows immigrants (regardless of status), survivors of domestic abuse, and returning citizens to obtain a driver's license. The legislation also prevents ICE (Immigration and Customs Enforcement) from accessing their personal information.[6]

To find a faith-based community organization near you, check out the IAF and Faith in Action websites.

Pope Francis had great respect for community organizations. In his 2020 book, *Let Us Dream: The Path to a Better Future*, he wrote:

> On the margins I have discovered so many social movements with roots in parishes or schools that bring people together to make them protagonists of their own histories, to set in motion dynamics that smacked of dignity. Taking life as it comes, they do not sit around resigned or complaining but come together to convert injustice into new possibilities. I call them "social poets." In mobilizing for change, in their search for dignity, I see a source of moral energy, a reserve of civic passion, capable of revitalizing our democracies and reorienting the economy.[7]

Poor People's Campaign

In 1968, the Southern Christian Leadership Conference (SCLC), led by Rev. Dr. Martin Luther King Jr., organized the Poor People's Campaign to call attention to poverty in America. The SCLC brought three thousand people together from a wide array of backgrounds. For six weeks, they camped on the Capitol Mall, demanding fair wages, affordable housing, and better education. Fifty thousand people then joined them in calling for an Economic Bill of Rights.

In 2018, fifty years after the original Poor People's Campaign, Bishop William Barber (an activist preacher based in North Carolina) and Dr. Liz Theoharis (a professor at Union Theological Seminary in New York) launched a new incarnation of the Poor People's Campaign. Although the organization is secular, both leaders are grounded in Christian theology. Their first action was to organize a wave of events and civil disobedience at state capitols across the country. They protested poverty, racism, and militarism and, in the process, built a national organization. They also conducted listening sessions with people living in poverty and low-wage earners across the country, shaping their policy agenda from what they heard.

The Poor People's Campaign organizes poor and low-wage people of all races in support of a broad social-change agenda. They estimate that 140 million people in the United States are either poor or earn low wages. People with higher incomes are welcome to help, but campaign events typically feature presentations by poor and low-wage people. The Poor People's Campaign is the most prominent current effort to bring the community organizing approach to the national level.

During the presidential election of 2020, then Vice President Biden agreed to speak to an assembly of the Poor People's Campaign. It was the best speech on poverty by a presidential candidate that I've heard. The plan he outlined became the basis for the American Rescue Plan Act in 2021, the bill that reduced child poverty to its lowest level ever.

During the first year of the second Trump administration, the Poor People's Campaign focused on Trump's legislative agenda. In May 2025, Rev. Barber sat on the steps of the US Capitol talking with Senator Cory Booker and House Minority Leader Hakeem Jeffries. They talked about religious faith and about Republican plans to shift massive public resources away from poor and working people to help fund tax cuts for wealthy people. Later that day, Barber was arrested for praying—without a permit—in the Capitol rotunda.

Meanwhile, Liz Theoharis was meeting with community organizing groups across the country about ways they can organize to meet growing needs for food and housing while also building power to push for policy change.

The Poor People's Campaign projects a radical vision of poor and low-income people rising up to demand radical, multifaceted social change. In a conversation with Liz when I was teaching at Union in 2021, she was clear that this may take a long time. "We have a fifty-year vision," she explained.

Labor Unions

Unions build solidarity among everyday people, creating a power base that protects them from abuse on the job. Unions also bring workers together to influence their wages, working conditions, and the benefits that make a job dignified and secure.

Unions play an important role in reducing poverty and boosting middle-class incomes. Workers in unions earn 25 to 30 percent more on average than nonunion workers, and states that have higher rates of unionization have lower poverty rates.[8] When unions secure improvements for union members, nonunionized companies need to compete for workers, so all workers benefit to some degree. When union membership was at its peak in the 1950s, about a third of US workers belonged to a union. Today, that number is dipping below 10 percent. This decline over the last four decades is one reason for the increase in income inequality during that period. The top 1 percent of income earners have gained larger and larger shares of total income: more than 22 percent in 2022.[9]

After the 2008 Great Recession, many states passed "right-to-work" laws that weakened unions. These laws ban union contracts from requiring all workers to pay dues or fees, even though unions must still represent them. This limits union funding and makes it harder to advocate for workers. A report from the Illinois Economic Policy Institute found that, eight years later, states with these laws had slower economic growth, lower wages, more debt, worse health outcomes, and less civic participation compared to states without such laws.[10]

It's not surprising that the generation experiencing the greatest economic uncertainty in decades is also the most pro-union. Gen Z (born between 1997 and 2012) is not only much more pro-union than older workers. Their support for organized labor cuts across educational, racial, and political lines.[11]

Young people have led some of the most visible union campaigns in recent years, including efforts at Starbucks and Amazon. In Buffalo, Starbucks baristas in their twenties launched the company's first successful unionization effort in 2021.[12] Since then, more than five hundred stores have voted to unionize. Organizers used digital tools such as social media and Zoom to coordinate their efforts. At Amazon, Chris Smalls and Derrick Palmer organized walkouts over unsafe conditions during the pandemic. After Smalls was fired, he launched the Amazon Labor Union, supported in part by a GoFundMe campaign. He and Palmer organized workers by meeting them at bus stops—sometimes bringing a cookout to start the conversation.[13]

Despite high-profile wins, union membership remains low—especially among Zoomers—and these new efforts face intense opposition. Both Starbucks and Amazon have been accused of union-busting, including firing organizers and delaying contract negotiations. US labor law gives employers significant advantages in resisting union efforts.[14] Still, young workers who are unafraid of disruption and savvy with the use of digital tools may help energize and strengthen labor unions and reshape the politics of poverty for a new generation.

Kim Bobo, a lifelong advocate for justice and author of a book on wage theft,[15] told me that supporting unions can be as simple as showing up. If you see people on strike, stop and ask why—they'll often welcome the solidarity. If you read about a strike, you might call the union and ask how you can help. Most cities also have a labor federation that meets regularly; reach out and see how you can get involved.

The Hard Core of the Poverty Abolition Movement

In Matthew Desmond's call for a poverty abolition movement, he was thinking mainly of groups such as those I've described in this chapter:

> Poverty will be abolished in America only when a mass movement demands it so. And today, such a movement stirs. American labor is once again on the move, growing more boisterous and feistier by the day, organizing workplaces once thought untouchable. A renewed movement for housing justice is gaining steam. In a resurgence of tenant power, renters have formed eviction blockades and chained themselves to the entrances of housing court, meeting the violence of displacement with a force of their own. The Poor People's Campaign has elevated the voices of low-income Americans around the country, voices challenging "the lie of scarcity in the midst of abundance" and mobilizing for things like educational equity and a reinvestment in public housing.[16]

Legislative advocacy, winning elections, and protecting democracy are also clearly important to the politics of poverty. The other strategies discussed in this book matter too. But people who both experience and push back against poverty and related injustices are the hard core of the poverty abolition movement.

Strategy 5
Charity and Business

This book argues that governments—especially the US federal government—are crucial to progress against poverty. But other institutions—notably charities, businesses, schools and universities, and the health care system—also play important roles in reducing poverty. This chapter celebrates what they do on behalf of people in need and argues that they can expand their impact by engaging in public policy advocacy.

I hope readers will think about the organizations in which they are involved—as a manager, employee, supporter, or customer. Is there an organization that might be more effective in helping people in poverty? Or one that is already helping poor people but might get involved in public policy advocacy? Institutional development requires sustained effort, but it can achieve durable improvements for people in need, including lasting changes in the politics of poverty.

This chapter begins with my experience at the Alliance to End Hunger, which works with charities, businesses, universities, health care institutions, and community groups. The chapter then focuses on three organizations—a charity and two businesses—that are effective in providing help and opportunity to people in poverty, in part through legislative advocacy.

The Alliance to End Hunger

My last assignment at the World Bank was helping the Bank engage with nongovernmental organizations around the world. So when I became president of Bread for the World in 1991, I saw our organization as one of many trying to reduce poverty. I hoped to expand Bread for the World's impact, but it was clear from the start that we needed to help build a broader movement to end hunger and poverty.

Richard Hoehn and I wrote a booklet called *Transforming the Politics of Hunger.* We used it to start conversations with other institutions and received the best responses from charities—both those that work in the United States and those that work around the world. I followed up with a number of possible partner organizations. Over time, the leadership of Feeding America, Catholic Charities, World Vision, and InterAction enlisted me to help them make the case to their boards and staff that they should get involved in advocacy. These are all very large charitable institutions and are now important partners in advocacy coalitions for hungry and poor people.

In 2001, Bread for the World convened a broad array of institutions— now including other anti-hunger advocacy organizations, diverse religious institutions, businesses, universities, health care networks, racial justice organizations, and labor unions. Together, we formed the Alliance to End Hunger.

Here are five examples of organizations in the Alliance that are helping to change the politics of poverty:

- The Alliance helped Islamic Relief engage its seventy thousand American Muslim members in advocacy on domestic and international hunger issues.

- DoorDash has partnered with food banks and others to deliver groceries—including "food as medicine" interventions—to families for whom transportation is a barrier. DoorDash is also working with advocates to make online grocery shopping using SNAP benefits a permanent option.

- The Alliance's Hunger Free Communities initiative helped the Indy Hunger Network mobilize the Indianapolis community to nearly end hunger in the city, in part by grassroots work to encourage people to enroll in the national nutrition programs.

- Auburn University set up the Hunger Free Alabama coalition (which showed up in Makensie Brown's story in the chapter on legislative advocacy, Strategy 1) and the Universities Fighting World Hunger Network, both of which include an advocacy focus.

- Rise Against Hunger provides volunteer-packaged meals to school feeding programs around the globe. Its association with the Alliance has helped the organization add a policy education dimension to its packaging events.

All these organizations evolved to have more impact, in part by engaging in legislative advocacy.

Eric Mitchell has succeeded me as president of the Alliance. It now includes about a hundred institutions and fifty Hunger Free Community Coalitions in communities across the country. The Alliance helps this network stay up to date and engaged in debates about US government policies that are important to progress against hunger. They speak out on issues together. It also serves as a coach and cheerleader as its member organizations move up the ladder of impact—from learning about public policy to participating in advocacy to leading coalitions of related institutions in advocacy.

If you are involved in a charity, business, or other organization that aspires to increase its social impact and is open to engaging in legislative advocacy, you might consider getting in touch with the Alliance to End Hunger.

Christ Church's Outreach Ministry

The rest of this chapter discusses three exemplary organizations: a local charity and two national corporations. They all illustrate what private institutions do to reduce poverty and human need—and how they can expand their impact through legislative advocacy. This section draws from the experience of the outreach ministry of the church I attend (Christ Church in Alexandria, Virginia). What has made it effective? How does it relate to government and to public policy advocacy?

Melanie Gray leads the outreach ministry of Christ Church. She is a trained social worker with years of experience. Our outreach ministry now includes fifteen programs that serve people in our community, Central America, and East Africa. Each of these programs is led by one or two lay leaders. Altogether, these ministries engage two hundred volunteers and receive financial contributions from about seven hundred sources (Christ Church members and others). They address the needs of about twelve thousand people in Alexandria each month, plus more than nine thousand people in Central America and East Africa.

Community organizations do some things that government programs can't—or can't do well. The connections between Christ Church volunteers and the people they serve are personal. One group of volunteers organizes a regular Bingo night with the elderly residents in a low-income housing development not far from the church. Another group supports an orphanage for girls in Honduras, and mission trips from Christ Church often visit them. The whole church sometimes prays for the girls by name on their birthdays.

Low-income and high-income families generally live in different neighborhoods, shop in different parts of town, and send their children to different schools. Christ Church's outreach ministry helps build a sense of community within the city and with people in far-off parts of the world.

Charity work is often spiritually enriching for volunteers and can be spiritually uplifting for clients as well. In a conversation I had with Melanie about Christ Church's outreach program, she told me, "For some of my volunteers, their time at the food pantry is more holy than church." She encourages her volunteers to cultivate empathy rather than sympathy. She wants them to think of themselves not as "doing for," but rather as "doing with"—or, better, "cheering on."

"Nobody wants to be 'a poor person,'" Melanie explained. "We want to partner with folks as they get on their feet." This is also good advice for those of us who focus on the politics of poverty.

Community organizations provide individualized care. A conversation with a mom who comes to a food pantry may lead to tutoring for one of her kids.

The best community organizations work in coalition with others. Melanie participates in weekly meetings with the city government and plays a leadership role within the faith community responding to emerging needs.

As Melanie discussed the work of Christ Church outreach, I was struck that Christ Church and other community organizations repeatedly have to respond to federal government actions. During the COVID pandemic, the federal government channeled money through state and local governments, which often channeled it through nonprofit community organizations. During that time, Christ Church played a major role in delivering rental assistance in Alexandria.

When the US government pulled out of Afghanistan in 2021, scores of refugee families came to Alexandria. Federal assistance to the refugees wasn't sufficient, and faith communities—including Christ Church—stepped forward to host forty-three refugee families. All of these families were able to become self-sufficient.

The influx of Afghan refugees included a seventeen-year-old boy who had been separated from his family in a crowd of desperate people in the Kabul airport. The State Department provided living assistance for three months.

This teenager enrolled in Alexandria City High School. Christ Church helped him find a job. He worked full-time, studied hard, and did well in school. He saved money and, with additional assistance from Christ Church, was able to help his family escape to Pakistan. He is now in college, still working full-time, and also advising other refugees.

In 2022, Melanie again played a leadership role among local churches, synagogues, and nonprofits in response to another crisis. As Congress ended pandemic assistance programs for renters, hundreds of families in Alexandria were confronted with eviction orders. The faith-community coalition decided to focus its resources on families who needed help paying back rent but could then manage their ongoing payments. Christ Church parishioners made it possible for a number of families to stay in their homes, and the faith-community coalition was able to provide financial assistance to more than six hundred people. But replacing all that the federal government had been doing was far more than the city government or the faith-community coalition could cover, so many of the poorest families were evicted, and some became homeless.

Christ Church has had a similar experience with one of its international partners, Mengo Hospital in Uganda. For over four decades, Mengo staff and Christ Church people have visited each other from time to time. In recent years, Christ Church has supported Mengo's HIV/AIDS clinic, which has been serving eight thousand patients. The primary source of funding for the clinic has been PEPFAR, the US government's program focused on HIV/AIDS. When the Trump administration abruptly stopped US international aid just after he came to power, the Mengo clinic had to lay off thirty staff. Christ Church provided $5,000 to pay salaries to the clinic's five remaining employees for one month, but church sources couldn't continue funding at the level the US government had been providing. Without a resumption of US funding, the clinic would have to close. Some patients might find help elsewhere, but many would die, and the HIV/AIDS pandemic would be likely to surge again in Uganda.

As discussed in the chapter on legislative advocacy (Strategy 1), the Senate restored a $400 million cut that the administration had made to PEPFAR.

Because of that victory in Congress, US funding for the Mengo HIV/AIDS clinic started up again in November 2025.

Christ Church has sometimes been involved in public policy advocacy. Christ Church has arranged meetings in Congress and the State Department for visiting African bishops. The youth group once studied SNAP and engaged many adults in joining them in advocacy with Congress in opposition to cuts in SNAP. Christ Church has repeatedly invited me to preach or lead adult forums. They also invited our representative in Congress, Don Beyer, to hold a townhall-style meeting between Sunday morning services.

Charities are important, and people who focus mainly on the politics of poverty should also engage directly with individuals and communities who are struggling with poverty—partly to ground ourselves and our thinking about policy in relationships with individuals and small groups. But it's also important for people who support charities to help change the politics of poverty. Churches and charities can't do it all; we need to ensure our government does its part.

To get a sense of just how much bigger government assistance programs are, the "big, beautiful bill" of 2025 cut $860 billion from Medicaid and $100 billion from SNAP food assistance. If churches tried to make up for this cut in the income of low-income people, each of the roughly 370,000 religious congregations in the country[1] would need to come up with $250,000 a year for the next ten years. I don't know of any church, synagogue, or mosque that could do that.

Chobani: A Case Study in Ethical Business Leadership

Businesses also play an important role in reducing poverty. They provide jobs—the most durable solution to poverty. They also provide goods and services that all of us (including low-income people) use. Some businesses are conscientious about how they treat their employees, about the intrinsic value of the goods and services they provide, and about the communities and nations in which they operate. Some of them sometimes use their influence with government officials to advance policies that address social concerns.

My first example of a corporation with a positive social impact is Chobani, the yogurt company. Max Finberg, who was the first director of the Alliance to End Hunger, now leads Chobani's government affairs department.

Chobani's annual profits are in the millions, and it holds close to a quarter of the market share for yogurt. But these achievements have not come at the expense of doing good. From the factory floor to Capitol Hill, Chobani is known as a mission-driven company—centered on the health and prosperity of people, rather than profit only.

According to Chobani's founder and CEO, Hamdi Ulukaya, "A cup of yogurt won't change the world, but how you make it might." He built his profitable business around the idea that doing good is good for business. He calls it a "return on kindness." Over and over, Ulukaya has shown that investing in people can help make a company successful.

Chobani produces protein-rich yogurt—an intrinsically good product. Chobani also treats its employees well: offering good jobs, fair wages, twelve weeks of paid parental leave, scholarships, and time off to volunteer. The company hires refugees and promotes pay equity. Ulukaya has also given employees partial ownership in the company.

Chobani is generous to people in need. Through its Community Impact Fund, the company has invested more than $1.8 million over seven years in projects to reduce poverty and make community improvements in the Idaho and New York cities where the company has plants.

During the pandemic, Chobani donated more than 10.5 million food products to schools, hospitals, and food banks. After Turkey was hit by an earthquake, Chobani developed a shelf-stable super milk that doesn't require refrigeration. The super milk is never sold; it is made available for disaster and hunger relief.

Chobani is also active in legislative advocacy, with a focus on child hunger and refugees. Chobani is part of the bipartisan WIC coalition that I wrote about in the chapter on legislative advocacy (Strategy 1). In 2024, the company placed an op-ed on WIC in *Fortune* magazine, signed by Hamdi Ulukaya and Jennifer Garner, a celebrity advocate. It elicited a surge of letters to Congress in support of adequate funding for WIC nutrition assistance.

Since Chobani has a plant in Idaho, it has developed a relationship with Senator Mike Crapo. Chobani's advocacy includes support for the Child Tax Credit (CTC), which reduces taxes in a way that incentivizes work for nearly all families with children and is one of the most effective policies for reducing poverty.

When Republicans became the majority party in 2025, Crapo became chair of the Senate Finance Committee, which has jurisdiction over tax policy. Crapo was invited to Chobani's plant in Idaho for a celebration of its expansion—a half-billion dollar investment that will create jobs and increase sales from Idaho's dairy farms. In a side meeting, Crapo met with Max Finberg and other advocates for the CTC, including Dawn Pierce (Strategy 1 again). Crapo told them that he had decided to push for the expansion of the CTC—also for poor working families—in the big tax package that Republicans were putting together. He confirmed this in a press interview the next day.

Trump's "big, beautiful bill" expanded the CTC for middle- and lower-middle-income families. This was the most progressive feature of the bill. But poor working families were left out. Advocates don't always get what we seek, and I appreciate Chobani's willingness to use its influence for children in poverty.

As consumers, we can favor good companies and shun exceptionally bad companies. Lots of people do this, and you might want to try Chobani yogurt.

John Driscoll and CareCentrix

John Driscoll is another corporate executive who is also a poverty abolitionist. He has been the CEO or board chair of several companies in the health care sector.

In 2014, he took over a troubled health care services company called CareCentrix. Entry-level employees were making the federal minimum wage of $7.25 (equivalent to $15,000 a year). Revenue was too low and staff turnover too high.

As the new CEO, he made sure that employees could reach him directly to introduce themselves and share thoughts about the company. He told me about one conversation with a customer service representative—a single mother with two small children who had lost her apartment and possessions in a fire. She said several times that she was "really sorry" to bother John but didn't have enough money to buy diapers. Could he possibly authorize an advance on her pay?

This woman's job was to visit people who had just left the hospital and check that they had enough food to eat and were taking their medications. This kind of personal attention reduces hospital readmission rates, and Medicare reduces what it pays to hospitals if too many patients return to the hospital soon after discharge. John's employee was doing valuable work but not making enough to care for her child's needs.

Conversations with a number of low-paid employees convinced John that CareCentrix couldn't maintain a stable and motivated staff without raising wages. He convinced the company's top twenty executives to give up their bonuses for one year and use that money to double their employees' base pay to $15 an hour. By freezing the wages of just twenty executives, CareCentrix was able to raise the wages of almost five hundred people.

Over the next ten years, CareCentrix's wages kept up with inflation. The company also provided affordable health care and bonuses to all employees.

These investments in people paid off for the company. It more than tripled in size and quadrupled in value before it was sold to Walgreens in 2022.

John Driscoll is also active in legislative advocacy, including work with a group called Patriotic Millionaires. They lobby for higher taxes for high-income people and a higher federal minimum wage. He is also active in the Democratic Party.[2]

Strategy 6

Defanging the Internet

The internet connects us with friends and family and with people on the other side of the world. It allows us to quickly find information—whether we want to know how to fix a tech problem or have a question about ancient history. The internet also offers an endless, mostly free stream of entertainment.

I didn't become proficient online until after my retirement from Bread for the World. As technology was becoming more important, colleagues at Bread handled that side of the organization and supported my involvement. But I retired during COVID and right away had to manage email, texts, and Zoom calls to stay connected. I went to Berkeley, California, to teach graduate students in the schools of theology and public policy, but my students and I were scattered all over the country. One student connected to our biweekly seminars from Nanjing, China. I had to learn fast about how to use digital tools.

I came to understand that online agility is the new literacy. It takes time and effort to learn how to read and write, but illiteracy closes doors to learning and makes it hard to share what you know. In the same way, older people who don't work hard to keep up with technology can't keep up with current ideas and innovations.

I came to appreciate social media. What I most like about it is that I get immediate feedback when I share an idea. If very few people open my post or read to the end of it, I know right away that I'm not communicating well. I also use Google searches and AI to help with research.

Because the internet is widely used, it is a powerful tool in the fight for economic justice. But it is also corrupting our politics and strengthening the forces that oppose the public policies that help families struggling with poverty. Defanging the internet means reclaiming it as a space of healthy social interaction. It also means strengthening the online participation of marginalized people and pro-justice voices.

The Power of the Internet

The internet, particularly via cell phones, has a prominent place in contemporary culture and certainly dominates the news media. Today's public square is online, and the public opinion that drives political action is shaped there.

The shift to digital media has radically changed how people access news and information. According to a 2024 Pew Research Center study, 86 percent of US adults sometimes get their news from a smartphone, computer, or tablet—and more than half say they do so regularly. Although a quarter of these people access online newspapers—often behind a paywall—more and more people (43 percent of those under the age of thirty) prefer getting their news from social media, podcasts, or Google searches—sources that don't cost anything but often lack verification and traditional journalistic oversight.[1]

In many ways, this is a positive shift. Knowledge is no longer limited to elites; people from all social and economic backgrounds can access information through their smartphones. The world is at their fingertips.

This shift has had a positive impact on civic engagement—encouraging more people to discuss politics and social issues, and perhaps contact elected officials.[2] Most advocacy organizations will help you to quickly send an email to your member of Congress from their website—often providing key information and prewritten messages to make engagement easier.

Increased access to information is one reason why more Americans have voted in recent elections. Much of the increase in voter participation has been among younger voters, who often have lower incomes.[3] In general, new voters have split their votes between Republicans and Democrats, with college-educated people more likely to vote for Democrats. Republican politicians now look to white working-class voters as part of their constituency, and politicians in both parties have become more alert to what young, lower-income Americans want.

Beyond influencing voter participation, the internet also facilitates social movements. We have already discussed how the #BlackLivesMatter hashtag launched a movement that still reverberates today. Social media gave a marginalized community a modern platform of resistance, amplifying their voices beyond what traditional media would have allowed.

There are many examples where the internet—and social media in particular—have been used to give historically silenced voices a platform. Women used #MeToo to expose the widespread reality of sexual harassment, leading to corporate reforms and new workplace protections. The short-lived Occupy Wall Street movement brought attention to economic inequality and corporate power in politics, although it had little impact on policy.

As Elon Musk's DOGE attacked government departments and agencies in the early weeks of 2025, people across the country flooded the internet and the offices of congressional Republicans with posts, emails, and phone calls—mostly in opposition to what was happening. In February 2025, senators were receiving 1,600 calls a minute, up from the usual forty calls a minute.[4]

Negative Effects

The internet has also had negative effects on us and our politics, notably widespread loneliness, sharp divisions in society, and manipulation by businesses and politicians.

Loneliness. Digital technologies connect people across time and space in ways never seen before. Friends, family, and even strangers can share ideas, images, and causes we care about on social media. But the more time we spend online rather than in real-life interactions, the less happy we are. A 2023 study found that increased social media use is linked to rising loneliness.[5] A Gallup survey found that teens now spend an average of five hours a day on social media.[6]

Neuroscientists have studied the effects of social media on the brain and found that it activates the same regions as addictive substances. Every like, comment, or notification delivers a small rush of dopamine, reinforcing compulsive use. Over time, this cycle can contribute to increased anxiety, depression, social withdrawal, and even cognitive decline.[7]

As applications of artificial intelligence develop, we can expect chatbots that are programmed to serve as therapists. Some people will connect with bots as if they were friends or even romantic partners, a path to loneliness for sure.

Division. Online interactions can also amplify hostility. Face-to-face communication includes nonverbal cues, which foster empathy and help regulate what we say. Digital communication filters out most nonverbal cues. We are less inclined to understand the other person's feelings and less inclined to self-edit offensive comments online.

Social networking sites may have been built to foster connection, but their core business is selling access to users. In 2025, the social media market was valued at $256.5 billion—an industry fueled almost entirely by digital ads. These platforms prioritize short-form content designed to capture attention by triggering emotional reactions. Algorithms—the automated formulas that dictate what users see—track user behavior and feed them content that is likely to keep them engaged.

Algorithms are proprietary—meaning the user never knows exactly what the rules are that determine what they see. These formulas may differ across platforms, but they all share a common goal: to maximize engagement by understanding our preferences. The more data they collect, the better they can predict what will hold attention—whether it's a product, a political message, or a controversy. Everything is optimized to exploit human psychology and reinforce habits that keep users coming back.

But algorithms do more than just hold our attention—they shape what we see and what we don't. If we don't interact with posts on certain topics—or if we hide them—the algorithm learns to filter them out, ensuring that we hear less from people who think differently. Conversely, if we engage with a misleading claim—like a false story about immigrants—the platform registers our interest and will feed us similar content in the future. The use of AI-driven algorithms will likely make feeds even more insular in the future.

When content that promotes outrage and fear goes viral, online echo chambers intensify it. Over time, this selective exposure narrows our worldview, reinforces our beliefs, and deepens ideological divides.

Manipulation. In today's economy, data is the most valuable currency. Whoever controls it holds enormous power. Billions of dollars flow through data-mining companies that collect vast amounts of information from online activity and sell it to advertisers, political campaigns, and even governments. We create the data, but Big Tech profits from it.

You are being tracked all the time. Every app you open, every website you visit, every email you read, and every privacy policy you accept gives companies access to your personal data. They can track your finances, age, purchasing history, location, political views—even your fears—and this process is often hidden from public scrutiny.

For example, when you open an email from a company, it probably contains a tracking pixel that attaches to your device—a kind of digital handshake. Without your knowledge, that pixel can collect data on your browsing habits, allowing companies to predict your behavior. If they determine you're a good candidate to buy their toothpaste, they can follow you across the internet, targeting you with personalized ads.

But not all data miners just want to sell you toothpaste. Some want to shape your worldview, manipulate your fears, and influence your political choices, which gives them greater control over public opinion and, ultimately, you.

The insidious exploitation of data came to the forefront of public consciousness with the 2018 exposure of Cambridge Analytica—a data-mining company involved in both the Brexit referendum and Donald Trump's 2016 presidential campaign.[8] As a spin-off of SCL Group—a British firm specializing in psychological warfare and influence operations—Cambridge Analytica amassed vast datasets to manipulate voter behavior.

Millions of Facebook profiles were harvested, allowing the company to analyze individuals' activities, interests, and emotional states. Groups were segmented into behavioral categories, and those labeled "persuadables" were microtargeted with tailored messaging designed to leverage psychological vulnerabilities. Whistleblower Christopher Wylie described their approach as exploiting people's "inner demons."[9]

In the case of Brexit, these individuals were fed content designed to stoke grievances, such as immigration fears and economic anxieties—often with disinformation. For example, Leave campaigners promoted the false claim that the UK sent £350 million to the EU every week, and that this money could instead be used to fund the National Health Service.

Normally, political campaigns typically focus on likely voters—people who have voted before. However, the Brexit campaign connected with lots of people who hadn't been politically active before. Data-driven messaging helped Leave campaigners exploit emotional triggers and psychological vulnerabilities of these disenfranchised voters, influencing sentiment and ultimately contributing to Britain's exit from the EU.

The 2016 Trump for President campaign also used Cambridge Analytica's voter data to microtarget ads aimed at discouraging Black voter turnout in key swing states.[10] Partly because of ads—ranging from negative portrayals of Hillary Clinton to messages promoting apathy—Black voter turnout dropped to its lowest level in twenty years.

The exposure of these practices led to the dissolution of Cambridge Analytica and significant fines for Facebook. Yet comprehensive measures to protect against data exploitation and disinformation remain limited, and internet-savvy political messaging is now mass-produced on an industrial scale.

The Cambridge Analytica scandal was just the tip of the iceberg in how data can be weaponized by bad actors. The development of artificial intelligence will make internet manipulation yet more powerful. We will see more and better disinformation campaigns. Deep fakes—videos that show people doing and saying things they would never do or say—will likely proliferate, making it harder to differentiate between truth and fiction.

A small number of tech billionaires are gaining unprecedented control over information, infrastructure, and political influence. Some of them have allied themselves with President Trump and, thus, against poor and vulnerable people. X owner Elon Musk led the way with contributions of $288 million in the final months of Trump's 2024 campaign. Others made big contributions to Trump's inaugural celebrations, and Trump gave tech billionaires prominent seats at his inauguration. Meta CEO Mark Zuckerberg, Amazon CEO Jeff Bezos, Google CEO Sundar Pichai, and X owner Elon Musk smiled for the cameras as the president took the oath of office. Earlier that day, Apple's Tim Cook and TikTok CEO Shou Zi Chew had private meetings with Trump. Sam Altman, OpenAI's CEO, was at the White House on Trump's first day in office.

These are some of the richest men in the world. They also control staggering amounts of personal data on US citizens and stand at the forefront of shaping the future of technology. Within the first one hundred days of the Trump administration, proposals emerged to loosen regulations, grant tax cuts, and award new government contracts to these billionaires. Their financial contributions and control over information platforms give them significant political leverage—shaping public narratives and influencing decisions that affect millions of Americans.

People on the Margins
of the Information Economy

Low-income and rural people often feel like they are on the margins of America, and that's partly because they are, in fact, on the margins of the internet. They don't feel the negative effects of the internet, but they do feel the negative effects of being left out.

People Who Don't Buy Much. The internet gathers vast amounts of information about most Americans—mainly about what we want to buy. Companies share our data with each other, creating a collective internet brain. But that brain doesn't know much about people who don't have much money to spend or who don't have access to broadband.

I've come to understand this problem thanks to Eric Sapp, the president of Public Democracy, who is a pioneer in using advanced technologies for good. His organization focuses on communication with communities that feel nobody is listening, ranging from low-income African Americans to conservative-leaning white people who feel they are disrespected by affluent elites. Public Democracy projects always start with careful listening.

For example, it partnered with a local health agency in Louisiana to enroll the first fully representative sample of Black Americans in vaccine trials. Historically, Black Americans have been underrepresented in clinical research, contributing to less effective health care for their community. To address this, Public Democracy used digital engagement tools—including dynamic, cross-device ads—to communicate with Black Americans in Louisiana. They focused on listening to reasons for distrust of medical care and helped design a responsive outreach program that allowed them to achieve a representative sample for vaccine trials.[11]

Public Democracy has made breakthroughs in reaching people in need of opioid treatment and public health services. They have also been able to secure dramatic increases in voter participation by communities of color.

But they aren't the only ones reaching these communities. Bad actors have also learned how. Because low-income and rural Americans often have fewer options for accessing reliable news, they are especially vulnerable to this kind of targeting.

Low-income and rural people are especially likely to get their news from free sources like social media. Subscriptions to reliable news sources like the *New York Times* are expensive. Conservative and foreign actors understand that poorer Americans—who are disproportionately racial and ethnic minorities—cannot afford to get past paywalls. As a result, Fox News and other right-wing publications create keyword-matching content outside of paywalls, drawing lower-income communities to their sites after "bouncing" from paid content. Fox News has used this strategy for over a decade, with a focus on content relevant to racial and ethnic minorities.

In a project for the US Census, Public Democracy found that Fox News is the top source of online national news for Black Americans living below the poverty line. Poor Black Americans are not intentionally turning on Fox after work; rather, Fox is courting them through mathematical algorithms.

But the math doesn't stop there. Because of indexing—the way platforms track user behavior and then rank and deliver content in feeds—these lower-income Black communities have become increasingly likely to see Newsmax and Breitbart in their social and online feeds—and before it was banned, RT, the Russian propaganda network. Meanwhile, they have become less likely to see more progressive news outlets.

Bridging the Digital Divide. Being excluded from digital infrastructure is just as damaging as being manipulated within it.

My wife and I are close friends with Bev and Gaylord Wilcox, a couple who live in rural Nebraska near a town called Wilmer. Zoom calls together are difficult due to poor internet connectivity. Lack of broadband also makes it difficult for anybody to run a business in the Wilmer area, one reason that all of our friends' children have left the area for better opportunities elsewhere.

As population has declined, many local institutions—churches, schools, and shops—have closed.

The Wilcoxes watch the news every morning on Fox and then on MS NEWS. "Fox and MS NEWS always disagree," Gaylord told me during one visit, "and I don't have faith in either one of them. How's a person in my situation supposed to know what's really going on?"

The bipartisan infrastructure bill of 2021 launched a plan to give everybody in the United States access to high-speed internet. For low-income families, the government negotiated and subsidized lower prices. There was huge demand, but Congress allowed the funding to run out in early 2024. For rural people, the bill authorized funding to deliver high-speed internet access via fiber-optic cables. It's the fastest, most reliable technology.

Fiber-optic cable infrastructure is finally under construction in the Wilmer area. But as of the time of this writing, the Trump administration has paused the broadband access program. It seems that they are likely to put more emphasis on broadband via satellite, which is slower and less reliable than fiber-optic cables. Defanging the internet means not only curbing its abuses but also ensuring that everyone, in every community, has equal access to the digital public square.

Digital Strategies for Poverty Abolitionists

Below is a brief discussion of public policies that would moderate the harmful effects of technology on us and our politics and a list of ways we as individuals can use the internet to help change the politics of poverty.

Ways the government might help. During the Biden administration, the US government took action to address the social media problems of loneliness, division, and manipulation. This included a Surgeon General report on loneliness as a public health emergency, pressure on tech companies to discourage disinformation and hate speech on their platforms, antitrust actions to promote competition in the tech sector, and a commitment to universal broadband.

The Trump administration pursued an antitrust suit against Google and is likely to continue efforts to make broadband available in rural areas. But the administration's main tech-related initiatives in its first year were massive investments in blockchain technology (a boost to Trump's blockchain business) and artificial intelligence.[12] We're unlikely to see major new efforts from this administration to address the problems related to social media that this chapter has highlighted.

What we can do as individuals. We can manage our own use of technology and its influence on other people.[13]

- **Talk about poverty and social justice online.** You are an influencer within your own network. Post articles, facts, and share stories about poverty in your feed. Let your friends know what you are doing to address poverty.

- **Counter false narratives**. Share verified information, report misinformation, and amplify the voices of experts and frontline organizations. If you are not sure if something is true, do some research.

- **Approach discussions with empathy.** No one is immune to misinformation. Recognizing our own vulnerability makes us better equipped to challenge it in others. Listen for the fears that drive disinformation, and respond with truth rather than outrage.

- **Protect your privacy.** Close background apps, review privacy settings, opt out of unnecessary data tracking, and learn how misinformation spreads.

- **Safeguard your own mental health.** Limit your time online to reduce exposure to toxic content. Take time for face-to-face connection with other people.

- **Learn more about the internet.** We can protect ourselves and use the web more skillfully as we learn more about it. Activists may be able to multiply their impact by using AI.

- **Consider moving to ethical providers, such as Bluesky (an open-source platform) or choosing local retail stores instead of Amazon.** We can vote with our consumer choices, and the market seems to be moving toward ethical providers.

- **Engage regularly with organizations dedicated to ending poverty** by following them online, sharing their content, and amplifying their messages. Your interactions—likes, shares, and reposts—help boost anti-poverty content in algorithms, increasing its reach. Most nonprofits don't have a lot of advertising dollars, so they need this kind of support.

- **Advocate with elected officials.** Every member of Congress and many state-level officials maintain an online presence. Follow their accounts, engage with their posts, and use opportunities to comment, emphasizing your commitment to ending poverty. Stay informed by subscribing to anti-poverty nonprofit emails for updates on online advocacy opportunities.

Understanding how to use digital tools in new ways is important to renewed progress against poverty. People of my generation have a hard time keeping up with change in the digital world. But for younger generations who grew up online, these tools are second nature. As noted earlier, young union organizers used social media and online tools to grow their organizations in new ways. We need more of that kind of innovation in the poverty abolition movement. If you are digitally savvy, I trust you will think of new ways to use online tools to help end poverty.

Strategy 7
Reaching Across the Divide

There have always been sharp political divisions in the United States.[1] But the political divide now is wide and bitter. The divide has deepened through decades of social change—the decline of churches and other institutions that once brought conservatives and liberals together; the rise of social media, cable news, and talk radio; more combative stances among elected leaders; and population movements. Americans now often choose to live in places that reflect their political views, so we have less contact with people with whom we disagree.

Neither party dominates, so we often suffer from gridlock, and we sometimes zig to the left after one election and zag to the right after the next. We will not be able to mount a sustained effort to resolve poverty—or any other major national or global challenge—without conservatives and progressives working together.

The damage inflicted by the ongoing MAGA movement has been profound. It must be stopped. But at the same time, poverty abolitionists need to find ways to live and work with people who don't agree with us. This will take time.

I want to suggest two strategies that poverty abolitionists can deploy to reach across the political divide: first, make it our business to stay connected with people on the other side of issues we care deeply about; and second, find ways to address legitimate right-wing grievances.

Connecting Across the Political Divide

We can begin with family and friends who see the world differently. Staying connected doesn't mean agreeing; it means refusing to let political differences dissolve personal bonds and trying to maintain a conversation about issues that we see differently.

We might go further by proactively seeking out relationships that cross political lines. One way to do this is by participating in organizations that include both progressive and conservative people—churches, civic groups, and sports leagues. Local politics is often less partisan than national politics. Progressives and conservatives are sometimes able to work together on issues such as stormwater drainage or traffic control near schools.

My successor at Bread for the World, Eugene Cho, has written about gracious involvement in civic affairs in his most recent book, titled *Thou Shalt Not Be a Jerk.*

"Disagreeing with someone's politics, views, religion, and ideology is never permission to harass or bully that person," he writes.[2] And later, "In a culture that prizes speaking up, there is courage, too, in quieting down and truly listening."[3]

"Wouldn't it be amazing," he writes, "if the world clearly saw Christians as embodying the great commandments to love God and love our neighbors?"[4]

Eugene's book is a good resource to use in church study groups. Another helpful resource, appropriate for both churches and other groups, is the Essential Partners' *Guide to Conversations Across the Partisan Divide.*[5]

Two Places of Connection in My Life

I have stayed connected with people from my childhood state of Nebraska. Conservative people are also part of the church to which I belong. My relationships over the years with Nebraskans and with fellow members of Christ Church illustrate the occasional strains and ongoing blessings of reaching across the political divide.

When I went to college at Yale during the years of Black Power and protests against the war in Vietnam, my thinking moved far to the left of what most people in Nebraska were thinking. Surprisingly, it was Stokely Carmichael, a leader of the Black Power movement, who encouraged me to reconnect with people back home. In a speech to a group of students about race and poverty, he said, "If you are white, don't come to our communities to solve the problem. You need to go back to your own communities to solve the problem."

When I graduated, Yale gave me a fellowship to spend a year in Ghana studying indigenous Pentecostal churches. My airline ticket allowed me to travel through Asia on the way to Ghana and through Europe on the way back home. I then decided to spend a year in Nebraska, traveling the state in my dad's Pontiac. I also led adult education courses on contemporary issues. I wanted to learn more about my home state and the roots of Nebraska conservatism.

A year later, I enrolled at Concordia Seminary in St. Louis. Rather than prepare myself to be a minister in a liberal church, I decided to remain connected to the very conservative church body in which I'd grown up: the Lutheran Church—Missouri Synod. The degree course included a year-long internship, and I was able to arrange an internship back in Nebraska.

One month before my graduation in 1974, the conservative wing of the Missouri Synod expelled moderates from leadership positions. That included the president and deans of my seminary. Few Missouri Synod congregations would employ any of the seminarians who sided with Concordia Seminary's faculty. This schism sent my life on a different trajectory than I had planned. But I have managed to stay in touch with family and friends in Nebraska.

In the chapter about defanging the internet (Insight 6), I wrote about our friends Bev and Gaylord Wilcox. I called them up early in the Trump administration to hear what they and other people in their area were thinking about it. "I'm glad to see that somebody is shaking things up in Washington," Gaylord said. "We've got to get the deficit under control. But I think they may be moving too fast." I agreed that getting the deficit under control is important, and Gaylord didn't disagree with my caveat—"not at the expense of poor people."

Christ Church and controversial issues. In the chapter on charities and businesses (Strategy 5), I talked about Christ Church's outreach ministry. I've also been impressed by how Christ Church has dealt with politically charged controversies over the years—first, regarding homosexuality and, later, our nation's history of racial injustice.

In mid-2004, the General Convention of the Episcopal Church voted to approve the election of Eugene Robinson as the bishop of New Hampshire. He was married to another man.

My son Andrew had come out as a gay man in 2002, as he was graduating from high school. He skipped church during the summer after his freshman year. But as he prepared to return to college, my wife, Janet, urged him to go to church with us just once. "Do it for your mother," she pleaded.

It turned out that two laypeople who had attended the General Convention were reporting back during the education hour that Sunday. One of them had voted against the consecration of Bishop Robinson—the church's first openly gay bishop—because he knew it would divide the Episcopal Church from its partner churches in Africa. A follow-up discussion was planned for the next Sunday, and Andrew was determined to speak.

Not many people at church knew that Andrew was gay. He was coming out to the church in a public way for the first time. He spoke in a thoughtful, considerate way. I think some people changed their attitudes about homosexuality when they heard Andrew speak. Because of Andrew's courage, this was no longer just a question of what they thought about an issue—it was a question of support for a young man who had grown up in their church.

People were seated at big round tables. Christ Church's rector, then the Rev. Pierce Klemmt, was not at church that Sunday. But his wife, Tuke, invited Andrew and my other son, John, to sit with her and her daughters. Later that week, Pierce left a voicemail on Andrew's cell phone, thanking him for helping the people of Christ Church learn about sexual diversity. Andrew kept Pierce's message on his phone for months. My guess is that Pierce's voicemail shared the Christian gospel with my son more effectively than any of Pierce's sermons ever did.

Christ Church followed up with many hours of discussion among the people of the parish. Most of us had never talked much about homosexuality, gay marriage, or gay clergy before. I remember a discussion at one of those big round tables in which a choir member came out. He said, "I've been part of this church for thirty years, but have never before been able to speak about this aspect of my life."

In the end, Christ Church's vestry decided to remain in the Episcopal Church. Several other big Episcopal churches in northern Virginia left the denomination, and a number of families decided to leave Christ Church. One of them had pledged a million dollars to a building project, and Christ Church lost that funding.

Yet over time, Christ Church recovered, partly because many people who began with reservations about the Episcopal Church's affirmation of a gay bishop decided to stay in the Christ Church community. Also, some gay and lesbian people joined the parish. Some people of color also joined the church, perhaps because it now felt more like what Strategy 8 of this book calls a "loving, justice-oriented church."

A decade later, our church dealt with another controversial issue. The Black Lives Matter movement swept the nation in 2013. A new rector, the Rev. Noelle York-Simmons, led a process of education at our church regarding the history of racial injustice nationwide and in our city. I learned from that process that Alexandria, Virginia, was the center of the domestic slave trade in the decades before the Civil War, and that it didn't fully integrate its public elementary schools until 1973.

Christ Church is a historic institution. George Washington was a member. Robert E. Lee, commander of the Confederate troops, was baptized at Christ Church. After Lee's death, Christ Church mounted stone plaques in honor of Washington and Lee at the front of the church, flanking the altar.

In 2017, white supremacists from across the nation came to Charlottesville, Virginia, for a big demonstration. A counterprotest formed in response. The confrontation became violent, resulting in thirty injuries and one death.

For some time, some Christ Church members had felt that we should take down the Washington and Lee plaques. Our rector led a long series of listening and discussion sessions. Everybody was repeatedly urged to express their thoughts on this question. In response to people who argued that we shouldn't try to erase history, the vestry decided to move rather than remove the plaques. They set up a museum-like space on the church campus.

Christ Church received some negative publicity, notably on Fox News. President Trump criticized Christ Church for moving the Washington plaque. The church also received threats of violence, and a police car parked outside during services for two months. A few long-term members decided to move to another church, but over time, Christ Church has grown, now including more young families and people of color.

On two hot-button social issues—gay rights and racial injustice—Christ Church took time to listen carefully to all its members. In the end, our leadership made tough ethical choices: to defend gay people and, later, to make our church more welcoming to people of color. But respectful listening minimized bitter division and helped the congregation move forward together.

Policies That Address Right-Wing Grievances

Personal relationships across the political divide are fundamental, but they will not be enough to restore a pattern of collaboration to our nation's politics. We'll need to respond substantively to grievances that are being voiced by the other side. Below are some suggestions for ways that politically progressive people might address right-wing grievances.

Economic frustration. Most importantly, we need to address the economic frustrations of working-class and middle-class people. Since 1970, the share of total US household income received by middle-income families has dropped from 62 percent to only 42 percent, while high-income households have expanded their share from 29 percent to 50 percent—a stark shift that underscores the growing concentration of economic gains at the top.[6,7]

The best solution to this issue is to raise more revenue from high-income people for public investments that would raise income for low- and middle-income people. The top tax rates used to be much higher than they are now, and capitalism didn't falter as a result.

President Joe Biden's catchphrase was right—"development from the bottom up and the middle out." In his first legislation as president, he proposed tax increases for very high-income people and corporations. But all congressional Republicans and a few Democrats voted against them. As a result, the deficit increased, contributing to increased inflation. Wage increases did not keep up with rising prices,[8] and working- and middle-class voters came to have a low view of Biden's management of the economy.[9]

Immigration. Refugees and other immigrants often need help when they first arrive, but over time, they boost the economy and pay more in taxes than they receive in benefits.[10] One study showed that immigration raises the overall level of wages over a five-year period.[11]

Yet many Americans were alarmed by the surge in immigration during the Biden administration. ICE agents encountered more than eight million people annually at the Mexican border during those years—four times as many as during Trump's first term.[12]

We need a bipartisan deal on immigration policy. Congress hasn't updated immigration policy since 1986. As a result, immigration judges are overwhelmed with impossible backlogs.[13] A reformed immigration system would include effective border management, facilitation of legal immigration, and humane treatment of all immigrants.

Rural revitalization. Rural America is hurting. Opportunities continue to shrink, and young people continue to leave for cities. Much of this problem could be resolved by legislation—in this case, a reformed version of the Farm Bill. US farm policies now direct the bulk of farm subsidies to the biggest farms—90 percent go to the largest 20 percent of farms. The top 1 percent receives 25 percent of the total subsidy. On the other hand, the Farm Bill provides minimal funding for rural development (small-town infrastructure, for example, or credit for small businesses). The agricultural interests that benefit from the current setup are powerful. But progressive groups might be able to work with conservative-leaning rural people to shift some funding from commodity subsidies to rural development.[14]

Racial tension. Federal law requires most employers to provide equal opportunity to all employees, not discriminating based on race, color, religion, sex, transgender status, or national origin. It also requires organizations that receive government assistance to practice affirmative action. Affirmative action includes targeted recruitment among disadvantaged groups and the use of goals or quotas to encourage representation. President Biden signed an executive order in 2021 to promote diversity, equity, and inclusion (DEI) within the federal government and organizations receiving government funding. That included affirming the value of diversity, ensuring fair treatment for everyone, and fostering a sense of belonging.

The second Trump administration dismantled federal government support for equal opportunity, affirmative action, DEI, and education about the history of discrimination in America. They looked for examples of discrimination against white people and used concern about antisemitism as justification for right-wing government control of student demonstrations in solidarity with Gaza and of universities in general.

Affirmative action has been the subject of ongoing debate and legal challenges. The Supreme Court ruled against race-based considerations in college admissions in 2023. Colleges can consider difficulties that an applicant has overcome, but they are not allowed to consider race per se.

Going forward, our goal should be to reverse Trump's overreach but, in the process, also be attentive to grievances among white people. Everyone—including white people—should have equal opportunity in employment. Educational programs about discrimination don't need to make people feel guilty for things that happened in previous generations.

Support for men and boys. We can—and must—continue fighting for gender equity. But that effort should also make space to address the specific struggles of men and boys. Loneliness, suicide, educational decline, and stagnant wages—especially among Black men—are urgent concerns. Many working-class fathers—nearly one in four, according to the US Census[15]—are disconnected from their children. Young men—now just 42 percent of college students, down from 47 percent in 2011—[16] are increasingly falling behind in life.

The strain of tough-guy masculinity that is part of the MAGA movement may offer a certain emotional appeal, but it doesn't solve these problems. Evidence-based policy solutions are needed—solutions that affirm both men and women.

Some readers may bristle at some of these suggestions, thinking that attention to right-wing grievances could pull focus from progressive priorities. That risk is real. But we can care about both racial justice *and* rural revitalization. We can fight poverty *and* support working- and middle-class families.

Addressing the grievances that have attracted most working- and middle-class voters to MAGA could be the very thing that unlocks a durable coalition for renewed progress against poverty.

Strategy 8

Love and Justice Churches

Since retiring from Bread, I've been learning and teaching about religion and politics at academic institutions. That has included a study of social science, especially survey data, about how patterns of religious practice and belief influence whether we are active in civic life and whether or not we support public policies that contribute to economic justice.

This and the next two chapters outline spiritual strategies to help change the politics of poverty. This chapter, Strategy 8, makes a data-based argument for joining a spiritual community, sketches the landscape of religion and spirituality in America, and recommends joining or helping to develop a loving, justice-oriented church. The next chapter, Strategy 9, notes that education and educated faith tend to make people more supportive of economic justice. It then explores the implications of this finding for action. The final strategy, Strategy 10, is my favorite. It turns out that faith in a forgiving God leads people to be more supportive of economic justice and progressive policies generally. Strategy 10 presents the data and outlines follow-up action.

Nobody decides what they believe about God, or what religious practices to pursue, on the basis of survey data alone. But empirical evidence about practices and beliefs that are associated with commitment to economic justice is instructive, especially if you believe that taking care of people in need is close to the heart of God or simply the right thing to do.

The Benefits and Risks of Going to Church

Churches, synagogues, and mosques share messages that many people around the world have understood, over centuries, to come from God. They urge us to believe that God cares for us. Even in dark times, they give us hope for our lives and for humanity. Over many years, social science has confirmed that participation in a religious congregation tends to make people more joyful.[1]

A Pew Research Center international study in 2019 on the social effects of religion found that religion tends to make people not only happier but also healthier and more active in civic affairs. The study found that participation in a congregation plays a key role in producing these positive effects of religion.[2]

I first learned about empirical studies of the social and political impact of religion from Robert Putnam and David Campbell in their 2010 book *American Grace*.[3] Putnam and Campbell pointed out that these positive effects don't, in general, depend on particular doctrines. They come mainly from being part of an ethically charged community. Our church friends encourage us to get involved in specific charitable and community activities. Individuals who pray by themselves in church and leave without talking to anybody may not get these benefits.

American Grace also noted, already in 2010, that churches were becoming more conservative. I managed to get Putnam and Campbell on the phone one Sunday afternoon. I asked whether the progressive social effects of people going to church outweighed the impact of many churches' conservative influence on people's attitudes. At that time, Bob Putnam thought churches, in general, were doing more good than harm in this respect. But as the next chapter reports, recent studies make that more questionable.

Specifically, I am appalled that most white Christians, including eight in ten white Evangelicals, voted for Donald Trump in 2016, 2020, and 2024.[4] Trump's policies and personal morality are frequently in tension with the Spirit of Christ.

A Quick Sketch of American Religious History

The landscape of American religion and spirituality is complicated. But a quick sketch of American religious history, with a focus on right-wing Christianity and the exodus from organized religion in recent decades, may help to make sense of it all and the options it presents.

My work at Bread for the World and the Circle of Protection has connected me to many Christians who work intensely and persistently against hunger and poverty. Not all, but most of these people are connected to ecumenical Protestant churches (denominations that belong to the National Council of Churches) or progressive Catholic parishes. I'm encouraged by the leadership of the ecumenical Protestant churches and by our last two popes, Francis and Leo XIV.

Right-wing Christianity. The many churches that stand in opposition to social justice have deep historical roots in America. Already in the eighteenth and nineteenth centuries, many church leaders taught that enslaving Africans and conquering Native Americans were ordained by God. American Christianity split on the slavery issue, with several Protestant church bodies dividing into separate bodies in the North and South. A few predominantly white church traditions opposed, or at least wanted to moderate, the worst effects of slavery. Most African Americans attended their own churches, which served their communities and opposed slavery.

American Protestantism was further divided early in the twentieth century by the fundamentalist–modernist controversy. Modernists felt that Christianity needed to take modern science seriously and address social problems. Fundamentalists stressed the inerrancy of the Bible, refused to believe what science had learned about human evolution, and wanted to keep "politics"—by which they meant social-justice politics—out of the churches.

Nearly all the Protestant church bodies adopted the modernist line. But many individual congregations—including thousands of nondenominational, independent congregations—adopted a fundamentalist point of view. Some fundamentalist congregations were loosely joined together in the Southern Baptist Convention. Others were connected with like-minded Christians by traveling revivalist preachers and newsletters—or later, by radio preachers and evangelistic offerings on the internet. Over time, the conservative wing of American Protestantism, including Midwestern conservative church bodies, came together in the modern Evangelical movement.

The Religious Right emerged in the 1980s. It started when Republican operatives joined together with two television preachers, Jerry Falwell and Pat Robertson, to form new organizations that mobilized conservative Christians around abortion and other issues. Falwell founded the Moral Majority in 1979, and Robertson established the Christian Coalition in 1987. In subsequent years, other right-wing Christian activist organizations formed. Together, they came to be known as the Religious Right.

They lobbied within the Republican Party against abortion and, later, gay marriage. Over time, growing numbers of conservative Catholics aligned with them. Then, during the 2010 elections, the Religious Right worked closely with the far-right "Tea Party" movement, which advocated for deep cuts in government spending and taxes. During the presidential elections of 2016, most of the leaders of the Religious Right preferred other candidates over Donald Trump. But after Trump won the Republican primary, they set aside their hesitations about his moral character and campaigned for him.[5] While progressive Christians have generally avoided identifying with either political party, the Religious Right became an important constituency within the Republican Party.

In recent years, Christian nationalism has been on the rise in response to the increasing religious and ethnic diversity of the United States. A 2023 study from the Public Religion Research Institute and Brookings found that 20 percent of all Americans believe that "God has called Christians to exercise dominion over all areas of American society." Twenty-seven percent believe that "the U.S. government should declare America a Christian nation."

Twenty-eight percent agree that "because things have gotten so far off track in this country, we need a leader who is willing to break some rules if that's what it takes to set things right."[6]

They got their wish in President Trump. Many of Trump's supporters came to believe that God anointed him to make America great again. But as my friend Jim Wallis points out in *The False White Gospel*, key tenets of white Christian nationalism are contrary to the teachings of the Bible. The Bible teaches us to love all people, for example, and that all kinds of people are made in the image of God.[7]

The people who attend conservative churches are usually admirable, moral people in their personal lives. Conservative people often give generously to charity. But political conservatives, including religiously inspired political conservatives, have generally come to support harsh policies toward poor and vulnerable people.

The Great Rejection of Organized Religion. Immigration from around the world since the 1960s has made the religious life of America much more diverse. Then in the first decades of this century, "religiously unaffiliated" became the fastest-growing category of spirituality in the country. Americans, especially young people, left organized religion in droves.[8]

Some religiously unafffiliated people were turned off by traditional teachings about abortion and LGBTQ+ identities. Some were turned off by right-wing preachers or by bishops who protected sexual predators. Most religiously unaffiliated people grew up in families that were nominally mainline Protestant but not very involved in church.[9] Many people stopped going to church during COVID-19 and never returned.

This trend plateaued in the early 2020s. But when asked about their religion, 24 percent of Americans now say "nothing in particular." Together with people who say they are atheist or agnostic, the percentage of religiously unaffiliated people is 36 percent—more than a third of all Americans.[10] The percentage is higher for younger generations: 39 percent for Gen X and 51 percent for Gen Z.[11]

About half of religiously unaffiliated individuals say that spirituality is very important to them. Choice and wellness are major themes in contemporary spirituality among Americans generally, but especially among religiously unaffiliated people. Most Americans, but especially religiously unaffiliated people, practice mix-and-match, often do-it-yourself spiritualities: prayer and meditation, weekends in the mountains, maybe the daily horoscope.[12] "Whatever works for you" has, to some extent, replaced religious community and tradition for most Americans.[13]

Jessica Grose, a *New York Times* columnist, did a series of articles on Americans distancing themselves from religion. She asked her readers to tell her about their experience now disconnected from organized religion. Seven thousand people wrote back, and their letters indicated that many still long for the supportive, intergenerational, and reliable community that houses of worship often provide. While nonreligious people may seek meaning and connection elsewhere, churches and other religious institutions uniquely offer a "one-stop shop" for social support, inherited wisdom, ritual, interdependence, and help in times of need.[14]

Finding or Helping to Develop
a Love-and-Justice Community

If you are not part of a church, you might want to check if there's a spiritual community in your area that would work for you. Many ministers, priests, and rabbis would be glad to share information about churches and synagogues in your area. Alignment with social justice is not the only criterion for choosing a spiritual community, of course. But if social justice is important to you, seek out a loving spiritual community that is committed to social justice.

If you are an atheist or agnostic, you may still be able to find a spiritual community where you find meaning in the worship and fellowship. Consider a Unitarian Universalist church or a congregation of the Ethical Society.

Greg Epstein is the Humanist Chaplain at Harvard University. His book, *Good Without God,* celebrates the spirituality of people who don't believe in God and still do all they can to make the world a better place. He writes: "We conclude that if the universe we live in does not have competent moral management, then so be it; we must become superintendents of our own lives." But Epstein is keenly aware that people outside religious communities have a harder time finding community, and that "being a good person in a vacuum is not a very satisfying experience." His book lists scores of organizations and programs that provide humanist resources, including rituals for special occasions and networks of local congregations.[15]

If you are already a member of a religious congregation, and you find it frustrating, you might consider checking out other congregations. Alternatively, you may want to stay put and help make your congregation stronger and more aligned with what you believe it should be.

Churches and other spiritual congregations depend heavily on volunteers to visit the sick and lonely, teach children, help people in their neighborhood, support adult education programs, and provide financial support. They also need social activists to help the congregation change the world for God. You wouldn't be reading this book if you weren't committed to progress against poverty, and a religious congregation is a great place to recruit and organize others to support our cause. You might invite a group within your congregation to meet together to discuss this book.

You may meet some resistance. There will be disagreements on specific issues—even something as basic as help for hungry people. Disagreements can lead to helpful discussions. Many people come to church for comfort, guidance for daily life, and the promise of life after death; they don't want to hear about social issues and dislike hearing anything about politics in church. You might be able to start with a discussion about why political issues are church-worthy topics. If someone raises a question about IRS rules related to houses of worship, draw from the resources discussed in Strategies 1 and 2.

It usually takes considerable diplomacy and persistence to get a congregation engaged in social action: steps include a go-ahead from clergy or a church committee, two or more people providing leadership as a team, a step-by-step process to provide people with information to deepen their involvement, and, finally, celebration of achievements.

Going through this process in a prayerful community often makes lasting changes in the hearts of the people involved and in the congregation. It's a powerful way to change the politics of poverty.

If just one in three of the readers of this book becomes an active member of a religious community that is pushing for social justice or take steps to strengthen their community's efforts on justice issues, that will have a significant impact on US politics.

Strategy 9

Educated Faith

I have found a book titled *America's Four Gods* by Paul Froese and Christopher Bader especially thought-provoking and helpful. Its analysis of survey data gave me a better understanding of how Americans experience God and how that affects our views about public policy.[1] Its findings also suggested ways we can develop religion and spirituality to make our nation's politics more generous.

Our Experience of God Shapes Our Politics

Froese leads the Baylor Institute for the Study of Religion. On the basis of hundreds of interviews, he and his colleagues categorized Americans based on two variables: the extent to which we think God is engaged or remote from the world, and the extent to which we imagine God as stern or forgiving.[2] They conducted a series of large surveys to track the distribution of Americans' beliefs on these two questions and on social and political issues.

When Froese met with my seminar at Union Theological Seminary in New York, he shared previously unpublished data that demonstrated two patterns in how our experience of God affects our support for poverty-reducing policies (reducing income and racial disparities, for example, or government-provided health insurance):

- Perhaps surprisingly, people who experience God as mainly remote from the world or nonexistent tend to be more supportive of economic justice than people who think that God intervenes actively—often miraculously—in human affairs. Notably, atheists are generally more supportive of economic justice policies than the 90 percent of Americans who believe in God or think there might be a God.

- People who experience God mainly as forgiving or permissive tend to be more supportive of economic justice than people who experience God as stern.[3]

Education and Educated Faith

The rest of this chapter is focused on the first of these two findings. Initially, this finding upset me. How can it be, I wondered, that atheists and people who feel remote from God are more supportive of poverty-reducing policies than people who experience God as very much present?

Three VTS seminarians (Richard Nelson, Casey Jones, and Mark Witte) helped me review other sources of data on religion and politics in America. Other studies are generally consistent with these Baylor findings. Notably, surveys that focus on religious affiliation show that people who don't identify with any religious tradition (atheists, agnostics, and people who check "None in Particular" when asked about their religious affiliation) are, in general, more liberal and more likely to vote Democratic than people who identify with a religious tradition. People who identify with a Christian tradition, especially white people, are likely to be conservative and vote Republican. People who identify as Jews, Muslims, or some other non-Christian tradition are also more likely to vote for Democrats than Christians.[4]

As I dug more deeply into *America's Four Gods*, I noted that people with higher levels of education are more likely to respect science, doubt religious teachings, and also to support anti-poverty policies. I also noted that *America's Four Gods* uses belief in miracles as an indicator of whether a person believes that God is engaged in the world. But educated people, whether they believe in God or not, are less inclined to believe in miracles. Reflecting on my own faith, I don't rule out the possibility of miracles, but I've learned from science that almost everything can be explained in terms of regularities in the physical world, probability, and human choice. God is very present in my life, but I celebrate the fact that God respects human freedom and generally lets nature take its course. I'm also convinced that we can use evidence and logic to change society for the better.

In the sections below, I'll discuss two lines of action that would, based on this analysis, lead toward stronger support for anti-poverty policies. First, we can cultivate educated faith and support education generally. Second, it makes sense for Christians to learn from and work together for social change with people of other faiths and no faiths.

Education, Defending Education, and the Politics of Poverty

Educated faith and the defense of education will help to build the political commitment we need to renew progress against poverty.

We can start with our own continuing education. I've shared my process of learning from sociological studies in some detail, partly as an example of continuing education. We'll be better citizens if we are always learning.

Parents educate their children and also influence their religious development. It's a once-in-a-lifetime opportunity to cultivate both faith and a passion for learning. Churches, synagogues, and mosques also play an important role in the religious education of children and youth, and the growing share of American families who don't go to church means that a growing share of American children are learning very little about religion. Teaching Sunday School can be a powerful, long-term strategy to educate the next generation about faith. Bible stories and *Jesus Loves Me* are foundational. But it is also important for both children and adults to reflect on the Big Bang, community problems, and political issues in church.[5]

We can also defend education and science in our society. Education is valuable for many reasons, but partly because critical thinking tends to make people more progressive on economic justice and other issues. It's no coincidence that education and science, as well as people in poverty, are now under attack in the United States. For years, right-wing activists have pushed school boards to purge libraries of books that acknowledge the history of racism in America or the differences in human sexuality. The second Trump administration has attacked universities, defunded scientific research, dismissed inconvenient data, and promoted public-health ideas that are not rigorously grounded in science. Resisting these assaults aligns with defending policies that provide help and opportunity to poor people.

A closing word: in today's America, many people resent elitism among well-educated and affluent people. We need to value education and protect our educational system, and, at the same time, remember that everyone, regardless of schooling, carries unique life experience and wisdom. Many people who don't finish college respect education and science and find ways to educate themselves. In any case, everyone deserves to be treated with respect, and everyone has a vote.

Learning and Working with People of All Faiths and No Faiths

I remain deeply rooted and confident in the truths of Christianity, and I'm inspired by the extraordinary works of mercy that many Christians pursue around the world. But I've been humbled by the fact that people of other faiths, atheists, and people who feel remote from God generally tend to be more committed to achieving big changes for poor people than Christians and people who feel that God is active in our lives and the world.

Jesus said, "By their fruits you will know them" (Matthew 7:16)—that is, the way to know true religion is by its moral impact. He also repeatedly found strong faith among groups that religious people in his society considered outsiders (the Centurion in Matthew 8:5–9, for example). I've always been eager to work with all kinds of people, but the Baylor findings have made me even more eager for dialogue and partnership with people of all faiths and no faith. Christian people like me have gifts to share, but we clearly also have a lot to learn.

The Episcopal Diocese of Texas is encouraging its churches to help initiate purposeful groups they call "missional communities." These groups include people from outside the church. They can focus on whatever purpose the participants find important—the holistic wellness of people in the group or a food truck for people in need. Each missional group is linked to a parish, but these groups aren't covert operations to recruit church members. They are generous strategies to support the spirituality—and perhaps social-justice commitments—of church people and religiously unaffiliated people together.[6]

It seems unlikely that churches, synagogues, mosques, and temples will reverse the dramatic decline in religious affiliation any time soon. But we may be able to find ways to accompany religiously unaffiliated people (including those who do not have college degrees), share our spiritual experiences with one another, and together seek to improve our lives and the world. Working together to reduce—and perhaps end poverty—can give us all purpose and peace of mind.

Let me close this chapter with a few paragraphs about how community in our religiously diverse culture is playing out in my own life.

Both of my adult sons are religiously unaffiliated. My older son, Andrew, is a loving family member and a generous friend to many. He has taught me a lot about good nutrition, fitness, and therapy. He seldom attends church, but when he comes to church with my wife and me, he takes communion. My younger son, John, and his wife belong to a Catholic church but go to church only for baptisms, weddings, and funerals. John has his own philosophy and religion, which increasingly include references to God and Jesus. Both of my sons are politically progressive. Andrew is understandably most passionate about gay rights, while John is discouraged by corruption in politics. My wife and I deeply love and admire our sons, and they love us. They respect the faith that sustains us, and their journeys are enriching ours.

I'm a Lutheran pastor but am now also part of the Virginia Theological Seminary (VTS) community. VTS provides more than 25 percent of the clergy of The Episcopal Church. A quarter of all new Episcopal clergy graduate from VTS. Faculty all affirm the Nicene Creed, and many people in the VTS community worship together four times every week. Seminarians learn about the Bible, Christian theology, and the Anglican tradition. But the curriculum also includes interfaith studies, philosophy, and science. Faculty and students come from many backgrounds in this country and around the world. Partly due to its open-mindedness, VTS has developed a strong emphasis on racial justice. It was the first educational institution in the country to pay reparations to the descendants of African American people who worked at the institution during slavery and segregation.

Finally, my reflection on the fact that church-going Christians are generally less likely to support anti-poverty policies than other Americans has shaped this book. I have addressed it to people of all faiths and no organizationally sponsored faith. We certainly won't end poverty in the United States, or do our part to end it around the world, if we don't work together with all kinds of people.

Strategy 10

Faith in a Forgiving God

Paul Froese's second major finding about our experience of God and the politics of poverty was that people who experience God as forgiving are more likely to be progressive on economic justice and other issues than people who imagine God as stern.

God's forgiving love for the world is foundational to Christian faith and to my commitment to economic justice, so this survey-based evidence immediately made all kinds of sense to me.

God's forgiving love for each of us and the world is a major theme of the whole Bible. When my children were little, I sometimes told them the stories of Adam and Eve, Abraham, Isaac, and Jacob as bedtime stories. My son John once noted, "All these stories are kinda the same." Indeed, all the Genesis ancestor stories are tales of moral failure and forgiveness.

This theme continues with the repeated failures of the people of Israel to live up to the Mosaic law. Israel is divided and then conquered, but the Lord forgives and brings the exiles back to rebuild Jerusalem. They are promised a wonderful future.

The Gospel of Luke (23:34) reports that Jesus on the cross asked God to forgive the people who were killing him. St. Paul's letters make up about half the New Testament, and a verse from his letter to the Ephesians is a good summary of his message: "For by grace you have been saved through faith... not because of good works" (Ephesians 2:8).

Christians experience the forgiving love of God through Jesus Christ's life, death, and resurrection. But the experience of God's forgiving love is not limited to Christianity and Judaism. Forgiveness also appears in other religions and secular humanism, in part because these traditions have been influenced by Christianity. Also, nature is forgiving—beautiful and bountiful for all. As Jesus put it, "The sun shines on good and evil people alike." (Mathew 5:45).

Yet the Baylor studies have found that nearly half of all Americans—more than half of all American Christians—imagine God as mainly stern—perhaps loving, but like a stern father who strictly enforces his rules.[1]

People who imagine God as a strict father are likely to feel bound by religious rules, doctrines, and ways of doing things. Yet Jesus was notorious for breaking the Sabbath rules to heal people (Luke 13:1–17). The main teaching of all St. Paul's epistles was that the life, death, and resurrection of Jesus Christ offer us forgiveness and life in his Spirit. We are freed from rules, traditions, and tribes—and energized to be creative agents of God's love (Galatians 5:1 and 23). The Baylor findings suggest that many Christians are missing out on the joyful freedom that the Christian gospel offers.

A book called *The Righteous Mind* by psychologist Jonathan Haidt argues that the political polarization of our country is based, in part, on two types of morality. One is grounded in traditional authority and rules. The other responds to the needs of people, whatever they may be. Rule-focused morality argues, for example, that marriage has always been between a man and a woman. People-focused morality responds to the needs and possibilities of LGBTQ+ people. Haidt stresses that people on both sides of such debates are good, conscientious people.[2] That's true, but the Christian gospel invites us to move from rule-based morality to a person-centered ethic.

People who imagine God as stern tend to have judgmental attitudes about poor people. A 2017 article by the *Washington Post* carried this jarring headline: "Christians are more than twice as likely to blame a person's poverty on lack of effort." It reported on a national survey conducted by the *Post* and the Kaiser Family Foundation. They found that Christians are twice as likely as nonreligious people to blame poverty on a lack of effort among poor people rather than on circumstances beyond a person's control. Evangelical Protestants are three times more likely to blame the poor for their poverty.[3]

The data on Americans' experience of God brings us to a startling conclusion: if more Americans experienced God as forgiving, our nation's politics would be more generous.

Sharing God's Embrace

Christian evangelism has converted many people. But more often, our families and other close relationships shape how we imagine God. Some people grow up in a home that teaches and practices love and forgiveness. My parents were loving Christian people, and I learned before I could talk that I was loved—and that Jesus was somehow part of that love. An early childhood experience of forgiving love may be the most important thing that parents can give their children. Forgiving love in a marriage can also be a way that people experience the transforming embrace of God. If a family prays together, it adds a transcendent dimension to their love for one another.

Churches are another medium through which people hear and experience the good news of God's love and forgiveness. The Christian message that God, the ultimate reality, loves humanity and intends good things for us cannot be confirmed with evidence. It is a matter of faith, and faith comes from hearing the message (Romans 10:17).

Lisa Kimball, who leads VTS's lifelong learning program, says that an effective church is like a funnel. At the wide end of the funnel, the church gets to know many people in different ways—community events, meeting people in the neighborhood, or when parents drop their children off for Sunday school. An effective church is welcoming, affirming, and offers opportunities for participation—that might include just coming in for coffee while the kids are at Sunday school. Over time, people in the church invite the participation of newcomers in one of the church's ministries—perhaps a social group for young adults, a Thursday-morning breakfast for neighbors in need, or a service trip to an orphanage in Honduras. In all these interactions, the church affirms that God loves us all—just as we are.

As people experience loving community, they may be drawn to attend church services. We need to hear again and again that God loves and forgives us. After people attend church for a while, they may want to learn more—to study what the church teaches and take part in educational events. At the tip of the funnel is a relatively small group of people who have been shaped by the gospel of God's forgiving love. They are likely to be active in changing the world for God, partly by sharing the gospel of God's love with others.

Again, Christianity doesn't have a monopoly on the experience of transcendent grace. Other religions, certainly Judaism, teach it. Most people believe that love is the best thing in life. Many people experience God's majesty and love in nature. Some people use therapy to learn self-love. As people experience love, they are likely to share it with others.

God's Forgiving Love for the World

In the process of writing this book, I noted that the books that Amazon shows on its Religion and Spirituality pages are mainly about individual faith or spirituality. Very few are about charity, let alone social change.

Biblically based Christian faith is about God's forgiving love for each of us and for the whole world. The Gospels of Matthew, Mark, and Luke are about the Kingdom of God coming into the world. John 3:16, the best-known verse in the New Testament, begins with "For God so loved the world"—not just individuals. Paul's letters teach that the resurrection of Jesus has changed the world, notably that the spiritual powers that compete with love have been discredited (Colossians 2:15–3:14). The New Testament offers hope of life with God after death, but also hope that God will make history turn out well for humanity (Romans 8:19–23; Revelation 21:1–5).

Whether you look to the Bible for spiritual insight or not, we are all, in fact, connected to the rest of humanity and the planet. What happens on the other side of the world affects us. Spirituality that focuses entirely on personal well-being is less robust and satisfying than spirituality that focuses on working for a better world.

SUMMARY AND PERSONAL REFLECTIONS

The Path Toward Ending Poverty Leads Us Closer to God

Summing Up

Here again are the five foundational insights I shared in the first five chapters of this book:

1. Poverty is a solvable problem. We made dramatic progress against poverty in recent decades, and all the activists working to revive progress against poverty give us reason for hope in our difficult time.

2. There is tremendous dynamism among people living in poverty. Many people and developing countries will find ways to make economic progress despite all the dysfunction in today's world.

3. The horrible suffering and damage that poverty causes make the case for reducing poverty compelling.

4. The US government is important to renewed progress against poverty, and Americans of faith and conscience can influence our government.

5. The policies of the second Trump administration are increasing
    poverty in our country and worldwide, but an alternative set of
    policies could get progress back on track. Progress against poverty is
    affordable and politically feasible.

These are the ten effective strategies to change the politics of poverty:

1. Lobby your members of Congress and other elected officials.
    Legislative advocacy can have a significant impact even in difficult
    political environments.

2. Elections shape the future, and we now urgently need to elect more
    Democrats to Congress. Religious congregations should urge their
    members to give time, money, and votes to good candidates.

3. Resist the current threat to the rule of law, American freedoms, and
    democracy. Some people will need to suffer to protect democracy.

4. Get involved with organizations that empower people who struggle
    to overcome poverty and injustice.

5. Urge an organization in which you are involved—perhaps a charity
    or business—to expand its impact by engaging in legislative
    advocacy.

6. Do your part to make the internet a more positive influence in our
    lives and politics.

7. Reach across the political divide. We need to listen and be responsive
    to what people on the other side are saying. We won't be able to make
    durable progress against poverty or on any other issue if we can't
    work together.

8. Help to change American religion and spirituality for the better.
    Consider joining a religious congregation that is loving and promotes

social justice. People who go to church tend to be happier, more charitable, and more active in civic affairs.

9. Cultivate educated faith in yourself and others, and defend educational institutions. Religious people can learn from and should work for a better world with people of all faiths and no faith.

10. Open yourself to faith in God's forgiving love for the world. Practice forgiving love in your family and participate in a church that stresses God's grace and forgiveness.

Before you put this book aside, take a bit of time to think about what you have learned and what you will do about it.

Poverty, Politics, and the Golden Rule

As this book comes to a close, I want to restate the ethical case for becoming a poverty abolitionist and then share my Christian, Bible-based motivation for a life of work to overcome poverty.

Virtually all people feel conscience-bound to treat other people as we would like to be treated. As shown in Figure 5, versions of the Golden Rule are taught in all the world's great religions. The US Declaration of Independence and the United Nations' Universal Declaration of Human Rights are secular echoes of the Golden Rule, now applied to how we organize society.

The world's experience in recent decades has made it clear that we don't have to put up with mass poverty anymore. We know how to eliminate nearly all poverty worldwide; the costs are manageable, and everyone would be better off if all people had enough to live in dignity. Therefore, the Golden Rule now requires more than assistance to people in need. It also requires us to work for the policy changes that would virtually end poverty.

For people of all religions and religiously unaffiliated people, changing the politics of poverty is sacred work.

Figure 5

THE GOLDEN RULE

Bahá'í Faith

Lay not on any soul a load that you would not wish to be laid upon you, and desire not for anyone the things you would not desire for yourself.
— Bahá'u'lláh, Gleanings

Buddhism

Treat not others in ways that you yourself would find hurtful.
— The Buddha, Udana-Varga 5.18

Christianity

In everything, do to others as you would have them do to you.
— Jesus, Matthew 7:12

Confucianism

One word which sums up the basis of all good conduct . . . loving kindness. Do not do unto others what you do not want done to yourself.
— Confucius, Analects 15.23

Hinduism

This is the sum of duty: do not do to others what would cause pain if done to you.
— Mahabharata 5:1517

Islam

Not one of you truly believes until you wish tor others what you wish for yourself.
— The Prophet Muhammad, Hadith

Jainism

One should treat all creatures in the world as one would like to be treated.
— Mahavira, Sutrakritanga 1.11.33

Judaism

What is hateful to you, do not do to your neighbour.
— Hillel, Talmud, Shabbath 31a

Native Spirituality

We are as much alive as we keep the earth alive.
— Chief Dan George

Sikhism

I am a stranger to no one; and no one is a stranger to me. Indeed, I am a friend to all.
— Guru Granth Sahib, p.1299

Taoism

Regard your neighbour's gain as your own gain and your neighbour's loss as your own loss.
—Lao Tzu, T'ai Shang Kan Ying P'ien, 213-218

Unitarianism

We affirm and promote respect for the interdependent web of all existence of which we are a part.
— Unitarian principle

Universal Declaration of Human Rights

All human beings are born free and equal in dignity and rights. They are endowed with reason and conscience and should act towards one another in a spirit of brotherhood.
— UN General Assembly, 1948

US Declaration of Independence

We hold these truths to be self-evident, that all men are created equal, that they are endowed by their Creator with certain unalienable Rights, that among these are Life, Liberty and the pursuit of Happiness.
— The Continental Congress, 1776

Zoroastrianism

Do not do unto others whatever is injurious to yourself.
— Shayast-na-Shayast 13.29

Source: Adapted from The Golden Rule Across the World's Religions: Paul McKenna (Scarboro Missions, 2000).

The Seminal Events of the Bible

The Hebrew Scriptures and the New Testament are both grounded in historical events: the liberation of the Israelites from slavery in Egypt and the death and resurrection of Jesus Christ. The poverty abolition movement draws inspiration from both of these seminal events in the Bible.

The Exodus. God did not send Moses to Pharaoh's court to take up a collection of canned goods and blankets. He sent Moses to Pharaoh to demand that he let the Israelite slaves go free. That great liberation shaped them—and their children, and their children's children—for thousands of years.

The law that Moses received from the Lord again and again expressed concern for the widow, the orphan, and the immigrant. For example:

> Do not deprive the foreigner or the fatherless of justice, or take the cloak of the widow as a loan guarantee. Remember that you were slaves in Egypt and the Lord your God redeemed you from there. That is why I command you to do this.
>
> When you are harvesting in your field and you overlook a sheaf, do not go back to get it. Leave it for the foreigner, the fatherless and the widow, so that the Lord your God may bless you in all the work of your hands.
>
> (Deuteronomy 24: 17–19)

The rest of the Old Testament, particularly Psalms and the prophets, also alludes frequently to the Exodus. The Exodus story is told and retold both to highlight Israel's unfaithfulness and to offer the promise of a greater deliverance in the future.

Hundreds of millions of people escaped from hunger and extreme poverty over the last several decades. In this respect, the world is a much better place now than it was when I was a young man. This is a contemporary echo of the biblical Exodus—a fresh revelation of the loving, liberating character of reality.[1]

Jesus. The seminal event of the New Testament is the life, death, and resurrection of Jesus.

His main message was, "The kingdom of God is at hand; repent and believe the gospel" (Mark 1:15). Jesus's vision of the kingdom of God, as defined by his sermon at the start of his public ministry, reflects the Hebrew experience of God as liberator:

The Spirit of the Lord is upon me, because he has anointed me to bring good news to the poor.

He has sent me to proclaim release to the captives and recovering of sight to the blind,

to set at liberty those who are oppressed,

To proclaim the year of the Lord's favor. (Luke 4:15–19)

Jesus healed the sick and fed the hungry. He forgave sins. He socialized with outcasts. He taught radical morality and parables about the coming kingdom. He criticized religious leaders for ritual legalism and for "devouring widows' houses" (Luke 20:47).

Jesus's ministry climaxed in a confrontation with the religious and civil authorities in Jerusalem. The Roman Empire extracted heavy taxes that left people without bread, landless, and burdened by debt. Local authorities, including King Herod in Galilee and the high priest and Sanhedrin in Jerusalem, collected the taxes and took a cut.[2]

Jesus was executed as a threat to this oppressive order. The religious leaders told Pilate:

We found this man perverting our nation. He opposed payment of taxes to Caesar and claims to be the Messiah, a king.

(Luke 23:2)

The authors of the four Gospels stress that none of Jesus's disciples stood up for him. They all fled for their own safety.

Three days after his crucifixion, Jesus appeared to the disciples alive again. Although they had abandoned him, he greeted them, "Peace be with you." He appeared repeatedly to his followers over a period of weeks. Then, after forty days, the Holy Spirit gripped his disciples. Their noisy ecstasy attracted a crowd, and Peter spoke to them. He said that they had killed God's Messiah, but that God raised Jesus from the dead to offer forgiveness and a Spirit-filled life to all people (Acts 2:37–39).

Jesus's disciples soon fanned out into all parts of the known world, preaching this gospel of forgiveness, Spirit-filled life, and the abiding hope for God's reign on earth. This message has given joy and hope to many billions of people over the centuries, both Christians and people beyond the boundaries of Christianity.

In Jesus Christ, I experience God's embrace and purpose. This provides powerful motivation to work for the abolition of poverty. I pray for divine intervention and God's Spirit among us to deliver us from this difficult time.

NOTES

Insight 1

1 World Bank, *Global Poverty Update and Outlook: Poverty, Prosperity, and Planet Report 2024,* 51, https://www.worldbank.org/en/publication/poverty-prosperity-and-planet; United States Census Bureau, Poverty in the United States, 2023, Table B2. Number and Percentage of People in Poverty Using the Supplemental Poverty Line, https://www.census.gov/library/publications/2024/demo/p60-283.html. For the 1967 estimate, Christopher Wimer, Ryan Vinh, Jiwan Lee, and Sophie Collyer, "2023 Poverty Rates in Historical Perspective," Center on Poverty and Social Policy at Columbia University, 2024, 7, https://povertycenter.columbia.edu/publication/2023-poverty-rates-in-historical-perspective

2 Matthew Desmond, *Poverty, by America* (Penguin Random House, 2023), 183.

3 Here and in this book's last chapters, I recall a few Bible passages as I remember them, in my own words. I include chapter and verse to confirm that I'm reflecting what they say accurately.

Insight 3

1 David Brady, Ulrich Kohler, and Hui Zheng, "Novel Estimates of Mortality Associated with Poverty in the US," *JAMA Network: JAMA Internal Medicine*, April 17, 2023, https://jamanetwork.com/journals/jamainternalmedicine/fullarticle/2804032?guestAccessKey=5e3c70e5-f175-43ef-8e31-b04942227ccd&utm_source=For_The_Media&utm_medium=referral&utm_campaign=ftm_links&utm_content=tfl&utm_term=041723

2 US Census, "National Poverty in America Awareness Month," January 2025, https://www.census.gov/newsroom/stories/poverty-awareness-month.html

3 Federal Reserve Board, "Report on the Economic Well-Being of U.S. Households in 2024–May 2025," https://www.federalreserve.gov/publications/2025-economic-well-being-of-us-households-in-2024-savings-and-investments.htm

4 Mark Rand, "Poverty Facts and Myths," Confronting Poverty, https://confrontingpoverty.org/poverty-facts-and-myths/most-americans-will-experience-poverty/

5   Matthew Desmond, *Poverty, by America* (Penguin, 2023), 18.

6   The World Bank, "Poverty," https://www.worldbank.org/en/topic/poverty/
overview#:~:text=Almost%20700%20million%20people%20around,day%2C%20
the%20extreme%20poverty%20line

7   Nga Thi Viet Nguyen and Xavier Devictor, "When Poverty Meets Fragility: Why the
Next Decade of Poverty Reduction Is at Stake," World Bank, June 24, 2025, 3, https://
blogs.worldbank.org/en/dev4peace/when-poverty-meets-fragility–why-the-next-
decade-of-global-pove

8   Nguyen and Devictor, "When Poverty Meets Fragility," 2–4.

9   The estimates of both chronic undernutrition and child malnutrition come from
https://www.fao.org/interactive/state-of-food-security-nutrition/en/

10   Global Network Against Food Crises, "Global Report on Food Crises," World Food
Programme, April 24, 2024, https://www.fsinplatform.org/report/global-report-food-
crises-2024/#acute-food-insecurity

11   Emi Suzuki and Haruna Kashiwase, "New UN Estimates Show 14,000 Children Die
Every Day Mostly of Preventable Causes," World Bank Blogs, January 9, 2023, https://
blogs.worldbank.org/opendata/new-un-estimates-show-14000-children-die-and-
5000-babies-are-stillborn-every-day-mostly

12   "2022 Disasters in Numbers," Reliefweb, UN Office for the Coordination of
Humanitarian Affairs, March 17, 2023, https://reliefweb.int/report/world/2022-
disasters-numbers

13   Deepa Narayan, Robert Chambers, Meera K. Shah, Patti Petesch, *Voices of the Poor:
Crying Out for Change* (Oxford University Press for the World Bank, 2000).

14   U2 Interference, "Transcript: Bono at the Prayer Breakfast," https://www.
u2interference.com/threads/transcript-bono-at-the-prayer-breakfast.153545/

Insight 4

1   Sheyda F. A. Jahanbani, *The Poverty of the World: Rediscovering the Poor at Home and
Abroad, 1941–1968* (Oxford University Press, 2023), 148–50.

2   Ryan Quinn, Bread for the World, "PFDA Funding Change over the Last Decade,"
private communication, January 6, 2023.

3   Bono, *Surrender* (Alfred A. Knopf, 2021), 353–557.

4   Julian E. Zelizer, *The Fierce Urgency of Now: Lyndon Johnson, Congress, and the Battle
for the Great Society* (Penguin, 2015).

5   Child Trends, "Lessons from a Historic Decline in Child Poverty," September 11, 2022, https://www.childtrends.org/publications/lessonsfrom-a-historic-decline-in-child-poverty

6   US Bureau of Labor Statistics, "Unemployment Rises in 2020, as the Country Battles the COVID-19 Pandemic," *Monthly Labor Review*, June 2021, https://www.bls.gov/opub/mlr/2021/article/unemployment-rises-in-2020-as-the-country-battles-the-covid-19-pandemic.htm

7   US Census Bureau, "Child Poverty Fell to Record Low 5.2% in 2021: Expansions of Child Tax Credit Contribute to Historic Decline in Child Poverty Since 2020," September 13, 2022, https://www.census.gov/library/stories/2022/09/record-drop-in-child-poverty.html

8   Center on Poverty and Social Policy at Columbia University, "Absence of Monthly Child Tax Credit Leads to 3.7 Million More People in Poverty in January 2022," https://www.povertycenter.columbia.edu/publication/monthly-poverty-january-2022; Center on Budget and Policy Priorities, "Record Rise in Poverty Highlights Importance of the Child Tax Credit," September 12, 2023, https://www.cbpp.org/press/statements/record-rise-in-poverty-highlights-importance-of-child-tax-credit-health-coverage

9   Ted Gittinger, "LBJ Champions the Civil Rights Act of 1964," *Prologue Magazine*, Summer 1964, https://www.archives.gov/publicationsprologue/2004/summer/civil-rights-act

Insight 5

1   World Food Programme, *2025 Global Outlook,* November 2024, 4–6, https://www.wfp.org/publications/wfp-2025-global-outlook

2   I highly recommend Matthew Desmond's *Poverty, by America.* But the analysis in *Poverty, by America* is guided by the old-style Census Bureau data, which doesn't count government assistance as income. That may be one reason why it puts less emphasis on government assistance, legislative advocacy, and elections than I do.

3   Economic Research Service, US Department of Agriculture, "Food Security in the U.S., 1/8/25," https://www.ers.usda.gov/topics/food-nutrition-assistance/food-security-in-the-us/key-statistics-graphics; and for global statistics, Food and Agriculture Organization, *The State of Food Security and Nutrition in the World 2024,* 2024, https://openknowledge.fao.org/items/7d387ffe-9c51-42b3-896a-bc16f128e525

Strategy 1

1   Turner, Seth. "Are Identical Mass Email Campaigns Effective?" LinkedIn, 1 June 2018, https://www.linkedin.com/pulse/identical-mass-email-campaigns-effective-seth-turner/

2   Bradford Fitch, Kathy Goldschmidt, and Nicole Folk Cooper, Citizen-Centric Advocacy: The Untapped Power of Constituent Engagement, Congressional Management Foundation, 2017. https://www.congressfoundation.org/storage/documents/CMF_Pubs/cmf-citizen-centric-advocacy.pdf

3   Sam Daley-Harris, *Reclaiming Democracy: Every Citizen's Guide to Transformational Advocacy* (Rivertown Books, 2024), 12–16 and 82–4.

4   IRS Publication 1828, "Tax Guide for Churches & Religious Organizations," 6–7, https://www.irs.gov/pub/irs-pdf/p1828.pdf.

5   Alliance for Justice, www.afj.org, see "Houses of Worship" in their resource library.

6   Ballotpedia, "State Government Trifectas," https://ballotpedia.org/State_government_trifectas

7   Interview with Kim Bobo, executive director, Virginia Interfaith Center, April 10, 2025.

8   Kristi Jacobson and Lori Silverbush, *A Place at the Table* (IMDbPro, 2014), https://www.imdb.com/title/tt1736049/

9   Barbie Isquierdo, *From Hunger to Hope: My Journey from Food Insecurity to Advocacy*, https://mail.google.com/mail/u/0/?tab=rm&ogbl#inbox/WhctKLbVlkFnVzGhzmNrLMlRwrzRmcMMGjNLhwNGHwXSqtwwt zPSJXcNJljk VfQNkcnQmdl?projector=1&messagePartId=0.1

Strategy 2

1   Aaron Earls, "Churchgoers Increasingly Prefer a Church That Shares Their Politics," *Lifeway Research*, November 1, 2022, https://research.lifeway.com/2022/11/01/churchgoers-increasingly-prefer-a-congregation-that-shares-their-politics/

2   Ballotpedia, "National Turnout Rates," https://ballotpedia.org/Voter_turnout_in_United_States_elections

3   Laurent Bouton, Julia Cagé, Edgard Dewitte, and Vincent Pons, "Small Campaign Donors," National Bureau of Economic Research, Revised 2024, 1–2. These researchers used data on contributions above $200 from the Federal Election

Commission, complemented by more comprehensive data from ActBlue and WinRed, https://www.nber.org/system/files/working_papers/w30050/w30050.pdf

4   Ryan Burge, "The Apathy Election: Political Engagement Dropped Dramatically in 2024," *Graphs About Religion*, Substack, June 30, 2025, https://religionunplugged.com/news/2025/7/1/the-apathy-election-political-engagement-dropped-dramatically-in-2024

5   Burge, "The Apathy Election," 15.

6   Jenn Hatfield, "More than 80% of Americans Believe Elected Officials Don't Care What People Like Them Think," Pew Research Center, April 30, 2024, https://www.pewresearch.org/short-reads/2024/04/30/more-than-80-of-americans-believe-elected-officials-dont-care-what-people-like-them-think/

7   Michael John Burton, William J. Miller, and Daniel M. Shea, *Campaign Craft* (Praeger, 2015), 122.

8   Robert G. Kaiser, *So Damn Much Money: The Triumph of Lobbying and the Corrosion of American Government* (Knopf, 2010).

9   This is crisply explained by Karl Everston-Hillstrom, "More Money, Less Transparency: A Decade Under Citizens United," January 14, 2020, https://www.opensecrets.org/news/reports/a-decade-under-citizens-united

10 Jimmy Cloutier, "Senate Democrats' Election Reform Bill Includes Campaign Finance Law Overhaul," Open Secrets, January 19, 2022, https://opensecretsnews.wpcomstaging.com/2022/01/senate-democrats-election-reform-overhaul-campaign-finance/

11 Bouton et al., "Small Campaign Donors," 1–2.

12 Burton, Miller, and Shea, *Campaign Craft,* 122.

13 James Sergio Crocker, "Gen Z Will Save Democracy: The Power of Young Voters in 2026 and 2028," *Eyes on the Oval*, February 25, 2025, https://eyesontheoval.substack.com/p/gen-z-will-save-democracy

14 IRS Publication 1828, "Tax Guide for Churches & Religious Organizations," 7–9, https://www.irs.gov/pub/irs-pdf/p1828.pdf.

Strategy 3

1   Sarah Repucci and Amy Slipowitz, "The Global Expansion of Authoritarian Rule," Freedom in the World 2022 (Freedom House, February 2022), https://freedomhouse.org/report/freedom-world/2022/global-expansion-authoritarian-rule

2   Rick Steves, *The Story of Fascism in Europe*, directed by Steve Cammarano, Cameron Hewitt, and Gene Openshaw (Edmonds, WA: Rick Steves's Europe, 2018), 56 min., https://www.ricksteves.com/watch-read-listen/video/tv-show/fascism.

3   Protect Democracy, *The Authoritarian Playbook: How Reporters Can Contextualize and Cover Authoritarian Threats as Distinct from Politics-as-Usual*, June 15, 2022, https://protectdemocracy.org/work/the-authoritarian-playbook/

4   Horizons Project, "The Pillars of Support Project," accessed April 8, 2025, https://horizonsproject.us/the-pillars-of-support-project-url/

5   David French, "To Save Democracy, Here's a Playbook That Works: Poland Pulled Back from an Authoritarian Slide. What Can the U.S. Learn from Its Nonpartisan Approach?" *New York Times*, April 2, 2025, https://www.nytimes.com/2025/04/02/opinion/poland-democracy-us.html

6   Maria J. Stephan and Julia Roig, "Combatting Authoritarianism: The Skills and Infrastructure Needed to Organize Across Difference," *Just Security*, January 27, 2022, https://www.justsecurity.org/79978/combatting-authoritarianism-the-skills-and-infrastructure-needed-to-organize-across-difference/

7   Carroll Doherty, Jocelyn Kiley, and Claudia Deane, "What Trump Supporters Believe and Expect," Pew Research Center, November 13, 2024, https://www.pewresearch.org/short-reads/2024/11/13/what-trump-supporters-believe-and-expect/

8   The Workers Circle, "Democracy Circles," accessed April 8, 2025, https://www.circle.org/democracycircles

9   https://www.targetfast.org/

10 Anti-Authoritarian Podcast, "*A Winning Strategy: Defending Democracy with Civil Resistance, with Maria Stephan*," featuring Maria Stephan, hosted by Scot Nakagawa and Sue Hyde, November 28, 2024, audio, 49:46, https://convergencemag.com/podcast/a-winning-strategy-defending-democracy-with-civil-resistance-with-maria-stephan/

Strategy 4

1   Black Lives Matter, "Our History," March 19, 2024, https://blacklivesmatter.com/our-history/

2   Neely Bardwell, "Trump's First 100 Days of His Second Administration Have Been Chaotic in Indian Country," *Native News Online*, April 28, 2025, https://nativenewsonline.net/currents/trump-s-first-100-days-of-his-second-administration-has-been-chaotic-for-indian-country

3   Alex Brown, "Tribes, Native Students Sue Feds over Education Cuts," Minnesota Reformer, March 11, 2025, https://minnesotareformer.com/2025/03/11/tribes-native-students-sue-feds-over-education-cuts/

4   Richard L. Wood and Brad R. Fulton, *A Shared Future* (University of Chicago Press, 2015). These numbers come from the biggest study of faith-based community organizing that was ever done. It was carried out in 2012.

5   Industrial Area Foundation, "Signature Accomplishments," https://www.industrialareasfoundation.org/signature_accomplishments, accessed May 6, 2025.

6   Faith in Action, "Faith in New Jersey Won!," https://faithinaction.org/our-work/victories/faith-in-new-jersey-won/, accessed May 6, 2025.

7   Pope Francis, *Let Us Dream: The Path to a Better Future* (Simon & Schuster, 2020), 120.

8   Tom VanHeuvelen and David Brady, "Research Shows Labor Unions Help Lower the Risk of Poverty," *The Conversation*, July 6, 2021, https://theconversation.com/research-shows-labor-unions-help-lower-the-risk-of-poverty-161050

9   Laura Feiveson, "Labor Unions and the U.S. Economy," US Department of Treasury, August 28, 2023, https://home.treasury.gov/news/featured-stories/labor-unions-and-the-us-economy

10   Frank Manzo and Robert Bruno, "Promoting Good Jobs and a Stronger Economy: How Free Collective-Bargaining States Outperform 'Right-to Work' States," Illinois Economic Policy Institute Report, February 9, 2021, https://illinois update.com/wp-content/uploads/2020/05/ilepi-pmcr-promoting-good-jobs-and-a-stronger-economy-final.pdf

11   Aurelia Glass, "What You Need to Know About Gen Z's Support for Unions," Center for American Progress, August 9, 2023, https://www.americanprogress.org/article/what-you-need-to-know-about-gen-zs-support-for-unions/

12   Elizabeth Garone, "How Gen Z Baristas Are Spreading the Starbucks Unionization Effort," *Time*, February 18, 2022, 12:39 PM EST, https://time.com/6148475/starbucks-union-organizers-gen-z/

13   Andrea Hsu and Alina Selyukh, "He Was Fired by Amazon 2 Years Ago. Now He's the Force Behind the Company's First Union," *NPR*, April 2, 2022, 7:56 AM ET, https://www.npr.org/2022/04/02/1090353185/amazon-union-chris-smalls-organizer-staten-island

14   John Logan, *Corporate Union Busting in Plain Sight: How Amazon, Starbucks, and Trader Joe's Crushed Dynamic Grassroots Worker Organizing, Economic Policy Institute,* January 28, 2025, https://www.epi.org/publication/corporate-union-busting/

15   Kim Bobo, *Wage Theft in America: Why Millions of Americans Are Not Getting Paid and What We Can Do About It* (The New Press, 2016).

16   Matthew Desmond, *Poverty, by America,* (Penguin Random House, 2023), 184–5.

Strategy 5

1   Hartford Institute for Religion Research, "Fast Facts on American Religion," https:// hirr.hartfordinternational.edu/fast-facts-on-american-religion/#:~:text=Hartford%20 Institute%20estimates%20there%20are,of%20384%2C000%20by%20Simon%20G, accessed 5/13/25.

2   John Driscoll, Morris Pearl, and The Patriotic Millionaires, *Pay the People: Why Fair Pay Is Good for Business and Great for America* (New Press, 2024).

Strategy 6

1   Pew Research Center, "News Platform Fact Sheet," https://www.pewresearch.org/ journalism/fact-sheet/news-platform-fact-sheet/

2   S. Boulianne, "Twenty Years of Digital Media Effects on Civic and Political Participation," *Communication Research* 47, no. 7 (2020): 947–66.

3   D. M. Ordway, "Young Voters and Colleges' Efforts to Boost Turnout," Harvard Kennedy School, Shorenstein Center on Media, Politics and Public Policy, October 31, 2024, https://journalistsresource.org/politics-and-government/young-voters-colleges-election-turnout-research/

4   M. C. Miller, "As Trump and Musk Upend Washington, Congressional Phones Can't Keep Up," *New York Times*, February 7, 2025, https://www.nytimes.com/2025/02/07/ us/politics/congressional-phone-lines-trump-musk.html

5   T. Bonsaksen, M. Ruffolo, D. Price, J. Leung, H. Thygesen, G. Lamph,… A. Ø. Geirdal, "Associations Between Social Media Use and Loneliness in a Cross-National Population: Do Motives for Social Media Use Matter?," *Health Psychology and Behavioral Medicine* 11, no. 1 (2023), https://doi.org/10.1080/21642850.2022.2158089

6   J. Rothwell, "Teens Spend an Average of 4.8 Hours on Social Media Per Day," Gallup, October 13, 2023, https://news.gallup.com/poll/512576/teens-spend-average-hours-social-media-per-day.aspx

7   M. Korte, "The Impact of the Digital Revolution on Human Brain and Behavior: Where Do We Stand?," *Dialogues in Clinical Neuroscience* 22, no. 2 (2020): 101–11, https://doi.org/10.31887/DCNS.2020.22.2/mkorte

8   K. Amer and J. Noujaim (Directors), *The Great Hack* [film], Netflix, 2019.

9   C. Cadwalladr and E. Graham-Harrison, "Revealed: 50 Million Facebook Profiles Harvested for Cambridge Analytica in Major Data Breach," *Guardian*, March 17,

2018, https://www.theguardian.com/news/2018/mar/17/cambridge-analytica-facebook-influence-us-election

10   E. Gunn, "British TV Investigation Shows How Trump 2016 Campaign Tamped Down Black Voters" *Wisconsin Examiner*, October 1, 2020, https://wisconsinexaminer.com/briefs/bbc-investigation-shows-how-trump-2016-campaign-tamped-down-black-voters/

11   Public Democracy America, "COVID Trial," https://www.publicdemocracyamerica.org/covid-trial

12   "Trump Announces a $500 Billion Commitment to AI Infrastructure Investment in the United States," CNNBusiness, January 21, 2025, https://www.cnn.com/2025/01/21/tech/openai-oracle-softbank-trump-ai-investment/index.html

13   Robin Stephenson was very helpful with this chapter and especially with this practical advice.

Strategy 7

1   John Meacham, *The Soul of America: The Battle for Our Better Angels* (Random House, 2018).

2   Cho, *Thou Shalt Not Be a Jerk* (David C. Cook), 58.

3   Cho, *Thou Shalt Not Be a Jerk*, 87.

4   Cho, *Thou Shalt Not Be a Jerk*, 61.

5   Essential Partners, "A Guide to Conversations Across the Partisan Divide," https://pardot.whatisessential.org/partisan-conversation-guide

6   Rakesh Kochhar, "The State of the American Middle Class," Pew Research Center, May 31, 2024, https://www.pewresearch.org/2024/05/31/the-state-of-the-american-middle-class/

7   Katharina Buchholz, "How America's Middle Class Is Shrinking [Infographic]," *Forbes*, April 21, 2023, https://www.forbes.com/sites/katharinabuchholz/2023/04/21/how-americas-middle-class-is-shrinking-infographic/

8   Private Enterprise Research Center, Texas A&M, "Inflation and Wages January 2021–January 2024: The Record for the Biden Administration," February 13, 2025, https://perc.tamu.edu/blog/2025/02/biden-admin-inflation.html

9   Jonathan Wisman, "How the Democrats Lost the Working Class," *New York Times*, January 4, 2025, https://www.nytimes.com/2025/01/04/us/politics/democrats-working-class.html

10   American Immigration Council, *Starting Anew: The Economic Impact of Refugees in America*, June 2023, https://www.americanimmigrationcouncil.org/research/economic-impact-refugees-america

11   Stephen J. Terry, Thomas Chaney, Konrad B. Burchardi, Lisa Tarquinio, and Tarek A. Hassan, *Immigration, Innovation, and Growth*, June 2024, https://websites.umich.edu/~sjterry/PaperIIG.pdf

12   Lucy Golden, "How Many Immigrants Have Crossed the Border Illegally," *BBC Verify*, September 25, 2024, https://www.bbc.com/news/articles/c0jp4xqx2z3o

13   TRAC, "Immigration Court Backlog: Overall Down, Asylum Backlog Up," *Transactional Records Access Clearinghouse*, March 20, 2025, https://tracreports.org/whatsnew/email.250320.html

14   Michael D. Farren and Gregory Fitton, "Government Failure in the Farm Bill," *Mercatus Center at George Mason University*, February 2, 2018, https://www.mercatus.org/research/policy-briefs/government-failure-farm-bill?utm

15   US Census Bureau, "Living Arrangements of Children: 1960 to Present," data visualization, November 7, 2024, https://www.census.gov/content/dam/Census/library/visualizations/time-series/demo/families-and-households/ch-1.pdf

16   Richard Fry, "Fewer Young Men Are in College, Especially at 4-Year Schools," Pew Research Center, December 18, 2023, https://www.pewresearch.org/short-reads/2023/12/18/fewer-young-men-are-in-college-especially-at-4-year-schools/

Strategy 8

1   David G. Meyers, *The Pursuit of Happiness: Discovering the Pathway to Fulfillment, Well-Being and Enduring Personal Joy* (William Morrow, 1993).

2   Pew Research Center, "Religion's Relationship to Happiness, Civic Engagement and Health Around the World," January 31, 2019, https://www.pewresearch.org/religion/2019/01/31/religions-relationship-to-happiness-civic-engagement-and-health-around-the-world/. Also see Penny Edgell Becker and Pawan H. Dhingra, "Religious Involvement and Volunteering," *Sociology of Religion* 62, no. 3 (2001): 315–35, https://doi.org/10.2307/3712353 and Robyn L. Driskel and Larry Lyon, "Assessing the Role of Religious Beliefs on Secular and Spiritual Behaviors," *Review of Religious Research* 52, no. 4, (2011): 286–404, http://www.jstor.org/stable/23055568

3   Robert Putnam and David Campbell, *Amderican Grace: How Religion United and Divides US* (Simon & Schuster, 2012).

4   Robert P. Jones, "What White Christians Have Wrought," *Time Magazine*, November 11, 2024, https/time.com/7174260/white-christianity-trump-election-essay/

5 Sarah Posner, *Unholy: Why White Evangelicals Now Worship at the Altar of Donald Trump* (Random House, 2020).

6 *A Christian Nation? Understanding the Threat of Christian Nationalism to American Democracy and Culture*, 4 and 23.

7 Jim Wallis, *The False White Gospel* (St. Martin's Essentials, 2024).

8 Tara Isabella Burton, *Strange Rites: New Religions for a Godless World* (Public Affairs, 2020), 16. This book was an eye-opener for me.

9 Burton, *Strange Rites*, 16.

10 Ryan Burge, "The Nones Have Hit a Ceiling: After Decades Non-Stop Increases, Non-Religious Americans Have Plateaued," *Graphs About Religion*, May 21, 2025, https://www.graphsaboutreligion.com/p/religion-in-2024-the-plateau-is-real

11 Ryan Burge, "Race, Generations, and American Religion in 2023," *Graphs About Religion*, October 26, 2023, https://www.graphsaboutreligion.com/p/race-generations-and-american-religion

12 Elizabeth Drescher, *Choosing Our Religion: The Spiritual Life of America's Nones* (Oxford University Press, 2016), 21–6.

13 The United States has come to include significant Muslim Hindu, and Buddhist communities. These are—like Judaism in America—largely ethnic communities. But all Americans are now exposed to non-Christian religions and sometimes incorporate their ideas and practices into their own lives. Meditation and yoga are examples.

14 Jessica Grose, "What Churches Offer That 'Nones' Still Long For," *New York Times*, June 28, 2025, https://www.nytimes.com/2023/06/28/opinion/religion-affiliation-community.html

15 Greg Epstein, *Good Without God: What a Billion Nonreligious People Believe* (Harper Collins, 2009).

Strategy 9

1 Paul Froese and Christopher Bader, *America's Four Gods: What We Say About God—and What That Says About Us* (Oxford University Press, Updated Edition, 2015).

2 Froese and Bader, *America's Four Gods*, 1–11.

3 Froese and Bader discuss this topic on pp. 107–24 of *America's Four Gods*. You can watch Froese's presentation to my class at https://www.youtube.com/watch?v=qnsKhZMY75o

4   Ryan Burge's books and social media are a rich source of data on the complex topic of religion and politics. His Twitter feed of April 5, 2025, showed that most white Catholics, most white mainline Protestants, and most white Evangelicals voted for Donald Trump in 2024. Burge has also found that people who identify as Jews, Muslims, or other non-Christian faiths tend to be more liberal than Christians. An August 18, 2025, Twitter feed focused on religiously unaffiliated people who identify as "nothing in particular." While people who check "atheist" or "agnostic" are likely to be highly educated, "nothing in particular" people are likely to have low levels of education. Like atheists and agnostics, they lean Democratic, but less strongly than atheists and agnostics, and they are relatively unlikely to vote. "2024 Election Post Mortem: Nothing in Particulars," August 18, 2025, *Religion in Graphs,* https://www. graphsaboutreligion.com/p/2024-election-post-mortem-nothing?utm_source=post-email-title&publication_id=1561197&post_id=163667457&utm_campaign=email-post-title&isFreemail=true&r=1mmpav&triedRedirect=true&utm_medium=email

5   I recommend *The Just Love Story Bible* by Jaqui Lewis and Shannon Daley-Harris (Beaming Books, 2025).

6   https://www.epicenter.org/missional

Strategy 10

1   Paul Froese and Christopher Bader, *America's Four Gods: What We Say About God—and What That Says About Us,* (Oxford University Press, Updated Edition, 2015), 21.

2   Jonathan Haidt, *The Righteous Mind* (Vintage Books, 2012).

3   Julie Zauzmer, "Christians Are More than Twice as Likely to Blame a Person's Poverty on Lack of Effort," *Washington Post,* August 3, 2017.

Summary and Personal Reflections

1   David Beckmann, *Exodus from Hunger* (Westminster John Knox Press, 2010).

2   Marcus Borg, *Jesus* (Harper One, 1989), 91. This is a super book. I'm also excited about Pope Leo's letter to all Christians, *Dilexi Te* ("I Have Loved You"), October 4, 2025. He provides a comprehensive overview of what the Bible, teachers of the early Church, monastic orders, and Catholic social teaching during the modern era teach about love for people in poverty.

INDEX